0049741

DATE DUE

MAR 04 1998	

BRODART, INC.   Cat. No. 23-221

CHINESE HOUSEHOLD FURNITURE

FROM EXAMPLES
SELECTED AND MEASURED BY
CAROLINE F. BIEBER AND BEATRICE M. KATES

PHOTOGRAPHS BY HEDDA HAMMER MORRISON

TEXT BY GEORGE N. KATES
CURATOR OF ORIENTAL ART, THE BROOKLYN MUSEUM

DOVER PUBLICATIONS, INC.
NEW YORK

Published in Canada by General Publishing Company, Ltd., 30 Lesmill Road, Don Mills, Toronto, Ontario.
Published in the United Kingdom by Constable and Company, Ltd., 10 Orange Street, London WC 2.

This Dover edition, first published in 1962, is an unabridged and unaltered republication of the work first published by Harper and Brothers in 1948.

Standard Book Number: 486-20958-X

Manufactured in the United States of America
Dover Publications, Inc.
180 Varick Street
New York, N. Y. 10014

Des meubles luisants,
Polis par les ans,
Décoreraient notre chambre;

. . .

Tout y parlerait
A l'âme en secret
Sa douce langue natale.

. . .

Là, tout n'est qu'ordre et beauté,
Luxe, calme et volupté.

CHARLES BAUDELAIRE
L'invitation au voyage

TABLE OF CONTENTS

PREFACE

THIS BOOK came about during the snows and fireside domesticity of a North Chinese winter, in the Peking of 1937–1938. Two women, one British, Miss Caroline Frances Bieber, and one American, my sister, Miss Beatrice M. Kates, found themselves there at leisure in what now seem vanished days of fabulous ease and physical comfort. In the beginning they had desired only to make a record of the best furniture they saw in the houses of their friends, other "foreigners"— as the Chinese call them—like themselves. Suddenly they were filled with the pleasant project of making a book from their gatherings.

The years just preceding had been an especially favorable time, as later events were to prove, in the history of foreign residence, generally, in the old capital of China. Antiforeign feeling, which was liable to burst out sporadically in the days following the Boxer Rebellion, was at that time and in that place almost completely nonexistent. Peking, in the gentleness of manner of its inhabitants, in their courtesy and their good humor, had become for those lucky enough to have found it a sunlit haven difficult to describe, superb for the enjoyment of the mere sweetness of existence, unlike anything they had known before or—of course—have ever been able to find since.

In this air of the grandeur and tranquillity of deserted palaces, and of life, in quiet courtyards, led exactly as each individual would have it for himself, the members of the

different European and American communities, unlike some
of their predecessors, had begun the cultivation of a new
taste. They started carefully to gather pieces of excellent,
simple furniture, to be used in its own Chinese setting, together with their own creature comforts of ampler heating,
"self-arriving water"—the Chinese phrase for plumbing—and
similar amenities. Nimble-witted servants helped in the
search, often feathering their own as well as their masters'
nests in one clever operation; and people bought, and had
restored for their use, many fine old pieces.

The chase had been going on, among connoisseurs, for
some time when these two ladies set about their project.
They found a third helper, invaluable for the project, in a
talented photographer, Hedda Hammer, and began their
search for the best in houses in many parts of the walled
city. The camera was ready to click once servants had hauled
the pieces selected to open courtyards, and—if possible—
had stretched cloth backings behind to isolate them from
irrelevant surroundings.

Conversation kept bringing to light new possibilities,
chits were sent back and forth by messengers, appointments
were made, the light observed, and finally the pictures were
made. They were practically all of Chinese pieces that seemed
to represent the best of an old tradition, safe in temporary
havens within the houses of members of the foreign colony.

It was little realized that this was to be a last call, that
spreading waves of war were eventually to roll into quiet
Peking, and that days of peril and woe were not to be ended
until these peaceful garnerings had been rudely scattered to
many parts of the earth. So these pictures—taken, to be sure,
when the shadow of future events had already begun to
darken the scene—have now the further value of a docu-

mentation that no longer can be enriched in any large measure until our own times have changed. As the venture progressed, work was hastened somewhat and standards of
selection were made a little less rigid. Yet this was also in the
interest of general completeness, and in consequence the 112
plates here shown do cover a broad and really representative
range.

Lacquer was excluded from the collection from the outset,
as another and already more familiar variety, and only pieces
of hardwood were represented. Further, in this latter
medium the goal was the general repertory of household
furniture, of high quality, saved from the wreck of the
old regime after the collapse of Ch'ing society in Peking.
Once retrieved, this was put into good condition again,
such as in general only the "foreigner" could achieve, with
his interest, his care, and also the powerful magic of the then
current rates of exchange to back him. No attempt was made
to include palace pieces, a range completely different in
scale, technique, and intention.

The text to these photographs made in Peking, where I
also happened to be during the years both before and after
they were made, I have myself added. I have not intended
that this should be a scholarly sinological comment, expressed
in a form and in terms accessible only to few; it has deliber-
ately been made to explain in the simplest way possible the
use and, above all, the great adaptability of the range of
this furniture as a whole, because it has seemed that this is,
at the moment, the paramount task. No one is perfectly
informed on many factual matters concerning Chinese
cabinetmaking which normally have been a part of the record
in the more time-conscious West. We ask many questions
too unlike those that spring in Chinese minds to be given

clear answers. Yet there has been such gross misconception as to what Chinese interiors of refinement actually looked like, especially those in private houses, and so much loose information has been given to a gullible public, that to reproduce these elements of the setting, with photographs of actual pieces explained, is surely the first necessary step.

Cultivated human nature, in its superior manifestations, has been through the centuries much alike the world over. The Chinese who were the original patrons of the now-forgotten cabinetmakers, and who first used the pieces illustrated in this book, had aspirations, a sense of the fitting, and standards of taste more nearly like our own today than the public in general has as yet realized. Here is the proof, since the objects speak eloquently for themselves; and here also is the suggestion of what we have to learn in this field from one of the great civilized traditions of the world. *Chinoiserie,* especially in its more flagrantly artificial forms, is a perennial manifestation that must be subdued and understood for the unstable fantasy that it is if behind it we wish to see the true, great China.

And so this book has come into being, the fruit of pleasant days that soon were gone forever, yet also days of an opportunity seized and fortunately used. The three women who created it together found and recorded the best of an era. It is they, also, who made the measurements and determined in so far as they were able the names of the woods used by the native cabinetmaker, as well as similar details by which each piece can permanently be identified.

The general introduction and the text to each plate, added by me only in this present year, have thus as their primary object to make clear how these pieces were designed, how they fitted into traditional Chinese life, and how today they can fit into our own. Such a wealth of sober and appropriate design, a legacy from times of relative stability, may add reasonableness and balance to our own creation in this field during years of transformation.

GEORGE N. KATES

The Brooklyn Museum
April 22, 1947

ORIGINS AND DEVELOPMENT

GROWTH OF WESTERN INTEREST

TO comprehend the life of a civilized people one must know something of its household furniture and the setting for its daily living. Cultivated man has become so inseparable from this "decoration of life," as the French phrase it, that one cannot understand him without sinking oneself into a realization of this relationship. Conversely, as soon as the conventions and implications both of formal and informal installation and the objects that comprise them are intimately understood, one is on the highway to a firm understanding of higher matters.

Now it is a fact to be noted that perhaps the last of all the varied manifestations of the millennial ranges of Chinese art to reach the appreciation of the Western public is Chinese furniture. Little attention, compared with that lavished on porcelains and bronzes, has been given to it either in European or American museums; and except for production in lacquer—not in hardwoods, which is to be the only range to be considered in this book—publication in any European language, until our own time, has been negligible. The Chinese, moreover, have not given much notice, in literature, to their own production.

1

So far as the West is concerned it is possible to account for this lack by realizing the general circumstances under which our knowledge of Chinese art has come to us. In modern times Westerners first touched only the south of the country, hundreds of miles in days of slow travel from the seat of the court, which had been for some five centuries far to the north, in Peking.

Contact, further, was made in the first instance largely by traders, who had no great interest in subtleties of taste. They wanted "curios," of course, to bring back from a land where these existed in fabulous variety; and when the Chinese had once discovered what was in demand, they accommodatingly purveyed it. This gave us, in clipper-ship days, much of what is still treasured in American houses; such objects as Canton china, or lacquer boxes and sewing-tables. These were obviously gifts such as could easily be stowed away in a sailing ship and brought home.

Even when relations became more mature, the furnishings of the imperial court were considered altogether the most precious and interesting, although in one sense these also were not typical of the best taste. For the virtuosity of certain palace pieces, "tribute wares" many of them, had resulted from the custom of presenting *chefs-d'oeuvre,* elaborations especially designed to exhibit a maximum of technical perfection—not for use but for display, not for daily living but for chambers of audience. We have thus for some time been equipped with plates showing imperial throne rooms; but we know curiously little of the actual appearance and furnishings of the cultivated, private household. Even as recently as our own late eighteenth century, much escapes us of the aspect of the private dwelling rooms, in traditional style, of the man of refinement and a certain amount of wealth under the old tradition.

This is certainly explicable enough: the grandest and the gaudiest always focus attention, certainly when they have become common property after the fall of a regime, and when even the casually curious can tread what was once forbidden ground. Furthermore, when Europeans finally established themselves permanently in Peking, during the last century, the structure of Chinese society did not make possible a merging of its upper strata in private and informal contact with highly cultivated Westerners, most of whom were birds of passage in the Diplomatic Corps. The two groups, except on formal occasions, kept to themselves. Consequently, while the structure and traditions of the Ch'ing dynasty social system were still, if not intact, at least recognizable, there was far less opportunity than would have existed between citizens of any two European countries, let us say, to learn each other's manners and habits.

Thus it came about that even after several centuries of contact, comparatively little was known of the vast range of normal furniture used in private Chinese households of taste and dignity to serve the needs of an educated and literary population. The revelation of this sensible and sober, at times almost startlingly plain, world of practical design—full of valuable hints and implications for our life in the West today—has come only in our own generation, after our recovery from the bad taste of the Victorian age, with its interest in Oriental "carved teak," which fitted in well with its own scheme of things.

The plates in this book therefore represent a much more normal range of household pieces, in polished hardwoods for the most part, and although some of them had counterparts in certain of the more private apartments of the Forbidden City, they are representative on the whole of what, before the old tradition waned, would have been found in private houses where means were ample and taste was good. They have about them an air of dignity and sobriety; and it is against this setting rather than the more elaborate one hitherto presented to the Western public that we must reconstruct our picture of China during the Ming (1368–1644) and Ch'ing (1644–1911) dynasties.

Later, as the Manchu line approached its end, there was to occur a lamentable slump within the structure of the Chinese pattern itself. The wealth that had made possible the creation of most of the pieces of furniture represented in this book seems simply to have given out; or—even graver—it was by this time often expended for the tawdriest and most tasteless third-rate European objects that were transported across the broad Pacific Ocean, to make more modern the houses of a decadent nobility that comprehended little and was able even less to maintain the high refinement of a neglected and now discredited traditional style.

So in China's recent, painful, and not very successful attempt to re-orient herself in a changed world, the tradition of centuries was broken; and only by a pious gathering of *disjecta membra* can we hope, piece by piece, to eke out the curiously slight existing literary documentation, and finally achieve a clearer picture of the superior Chinese household in days of refinement and ease.

THE CHINESE TRADITION

The collection of photographs here reproduced was made, of course, by Westerners living in Peking, and is entirely composed of pieces belonging to themselves or to other "foreigners" living there about a decade ago. They represent not necessarily furniture originally made in the old capital, but at least and in all cases furniture found or used there.

It is not that similar pieces could not also on occasion turn up in Central or even South China. Indeed it may be that many of them were originally made there. The old furniture dealers of Peking used to call all good cabinet work *kuang tso,* or "Kuangtung manufacture," and give the name of *ching tso,* or "Capital make," surprisingly enough, to pieces of inferior technical excellence—explaining that when furniture was wanted to refurbish an apartment in a local palace when such a circumstance as the death of a former master might require prompt rearrangement, only then were pieces rather hastily put together under the direction of local cabinetmakers. Otherwise, they were made in the good days, we are told, in the South.

This statement is in itself surprising, and very difficult of proof; perhaps it is merely an inaccurate later trade use of two terms, which long ago applied literally to two general types of joinery. Yet it must not be forgotten that the precious woods themselves often came from outside the borders of the old Empire—and even from as far away, it is said, as the coasts of Indo-China and India—to the ports of the South. There the sea-borne logs could have been dressed, and perhaps actually fashioned into pieces of furniture, which then may slowly have been transported by way of the Grand Canal finally to Peking itself. This was never a range of furniture production for general use, even in days of great prosperity. Such luxury, sober though it may be, in Asia could not be for the millions.

Here, as almost everywhere in the analysis of things Chinese, we gradually become aware that misconception born of distance and of the ever-varying yet ever-constant legend of a happy, philosopher's land, where everything is better than at home, has also been at work. In any period the head of a large Chinese family who could afford himself the luxury of a complete and elegant installation, in harmonious styles and in polished hardwoods, must have been rare. Yet it was the ideal; and when the rich family par excellence of all Chinese novels is described, the Chia family in the eighteenth century *Dream of the Red Chamber*, it is furniture such as in this book that is alluded to, and occasionally described. Their dwellings were in Peking, the capital, in a climate with severe winters; and there the need of warm *k'angs*, or raised and heated brick platforms, which are such a special feature of North Chinese architecture, naturally led to quite different types of furniture from those appropriate, let us say, much farther to the south, in an open lakeside villa for summer residence in Hangchow or some bird-frequented, foliage-filled garden in aristocratic, tranquil Soochow.

Until much more scholarly work can be done, therefore, to determine the scope of local differences within the old tradition (a labor now doubly difficult since so many of the old settings, and all that composed them, were over the years appallingly degraded, and now in large numbers have vanished in unhappy China's perennial wars), until this slow labor can be undertaken and successfully concluded, one must be very cautious before labeling pieces definitely Northern or Southern. It is true, however, that the ordinary furniture and all the decorative arts of Southern China are in general much more elaborate in design, color, and material than what was conceived fitting in the more sober North.

WHAT THE WEST NOTICED

Further, as we have already seen, until almost our own time it was precisely the phases of Chinese culture dealing with private life, in a setting created by private wealth, that escaped Western notice almost entirely. This is specially true of furniture. It was not that China, in this one field only, failed to exert her perennial charm or to display the riches of her genius, the attraction of which continued in Europe to produce, unfailingly, generation after generation, changing forms of imitative *chinoiserie*. In the borrowing of furniture models, in the seventeenth and eighteenth centuries, certain varieties of the Chinese style had become even commonplace. The name of Chippendale at once comes to mind.

Yet the furniture noticed by such a contemporary, eighteenth-century Western designer as Chambers, for example, was often what, by exuberant contrast, was most surprisingly different from his own norms,[1] or later what was grandest and most overwhelming at the court. The latter was as partial and inaccurate an expression of the life of the average Chinese as, to use a rough example, was probably the fashionable, imported setting of the court of eighteenth-century Spain that of a contemporary hidalgo. Westerners, originally, far to the south, and later even in Peking, the capital, had practically no opportunity whatsoever of penetrating Chinese homes; indeed that side of Chinese life was, by intention, as completely as possible withheld from them. When considerably later, moreover, this barrier was at least in a measure lowered (for certain individuals) , the grand tradition had sadly declined. The sympathetic student of today can only trace imperfectly, by the use of such objects as have survived, the development of a style apparently in full flowering during a period of great prosperity in what corresponds roughly to our sixteenth, seventeenth, and eighteenth centuries. Practically nothing is left of furnishings belonging to periods earlier than this except the gutted shells of the architectural settings. The wear and tear of Asia, where teeming populations, in a time of commotion, strip like locusts anything left unprotected, furnishes the explanation.

Further, for a variety of causes—trader's ignorance, merchant's guile, or dealer's cleverness—collectors in the West had long been in the habit of calling "Chinese furniture," as if the term were all-inclusive, such elaborate examples in lacquer as had come out of China through loot or trade in the past century; they almost wholly ignored the more sober range of elegant hardwood that forms the subject matter of the present book. Yet it is plain, seasoned wood rather than other and more elaborate materials that traditionally was used for the general range of the best household pieces. To be sure, lacquer was often employed in a rich setting, especially when an effect of sumptuousness was desired, yet seldom, apparently, were whole installations made of it alone, except in palaces, unless perhaps for a few exceptional rooms.

All the general forms of the furniture here illustrated were also common enough in humbler materials in the poorest houses. Yet they could only be translated into terms of precious woods, with the refinement that these plates make clear, in those of the wealthy. The rarity and costliness of the best *tzu-t'an* (blackwood) or *hua-li* (rosewood) alone—we shall discuss these cabinet woods later in some detail—in large measure account for the fact that this range was never a common one. Indeed, with all Peking—that mine of the antiquarian—to draw on, it was not easy to procure the most superior pieces even a decade ago; and today it must be even more difficult. Many of them must have been connoisseurs' items even for the Chinese. Yet in their sobriety and elegance they express more clearly than examples in any other medium the basic intention behind all furniture design in China; and as such, for our purposes, they are standard.

NATIVE APPRAISALS

In our attempt to establish any detailed history of this important range of the Chinese craftsman's accomplishment, we obtain a minimum of help from the Chinese themselves. They never seem to have regarded the cabinetmaker as entitled to the artistic recognition freely accorded the calligrapher, for example, or the artist in general. Inscribed stones, bronzes, jades, moneys, mirrors—all these have long been highly prized and publicly esteemed. The various schools of ceramics, also, though the workers remain anonymous, have traditionally been carefully analyzed and classified.

Yet Chinese furniture has received, even in the typical Chinese encyclopaedias or local gazetteers—aiming in their enormous bulk at universality—so little attention down the centuries as to amount to practically nothing. It is difficult to find more than a mere handful of woodcut illustrations, even these summarily drawn, in all the range of such books.

The reason seems to be that the cabinetmaker was considered an artisan, not an artist. The legendary figures of P'an Ku and Lu Pan, the first carpenters, come to mind, of course, for here were craftsmen who attained divinity. Yet once the invention of working in wood had been ascribed to legendary figures of gigantic and shadowy proportions, the Chinese seem to have concerned themselves very little with their later successors. In the whole unbroken record of the Chinese dynastic histories, I do not know of a single mention of an outstanding cabinetmaker as an artist, in our sense of the word. All the extraordinary skill of his joinery, all the sensitiveness and refinement of his design, were maintained in anonymity. A craftsman or artisan, his work was considered a humble contribution within a grander scheme.

Another fact gravely hampers the inquiring student in this field. Destruction of property in China down the ages has been enormous, as all those who have lived in that country—with an active population, in great need, at times tugging frantically at limited resources for mere survival—well know. Political crises have also periodically overturned the established order, and in such times of upheaval the extrinsic value of objects, in ignorant hands, has often been far more obvious than their intrinsic worth. In quantity, so little furniture from dynasties before the Ming and Ch'ing has survived that the lack of materials to work with is disconcerting. With tremendous social pressure on the means of subsistence, even in ordinary times, what hope can there have been for the preservation of costly furniture, which is difficult to safeguard in time of peril or flight, perishable, and further, usable by all men?

We may therefore be quite sure that, as in so many other fields of Chinese art, in days of calamity objects of the greatest beauty were degraded, and often ruthlessly broken up, to give a modicum of immediate use to those in desperation. Quite apart from the vast amount destroyed in the periodic sack and burning of great palaces, such as quite regularly occurred at the end of dynasties, quantities also must have perished in minor upheavals, at times when public safety temporarily vanished. The vicissitudes of China's very troubled history in the nineteenth century must further be remembered. It is a memorable fact that not a single piece earlier than the Sung period—represented by the ruin of a single table and chair to be discussed later—has come down to us in China itself. Certain examples illustrated in this book, carefully restored to their original luster and beauty, which was possible because of their excellent and seasoned wood, were found half smashed, wrecked, and seemingly ruined, often unthinkingly exposed to the elements, no longer considered of much use by the ignorant. Credit for a part of this work of reconstruction therefore is due to the Westerner, whose curiosity and persistence have here brought tangible results. One must have seen many of these pieces when they were first rescued to know to how low a state some of them had been allowed to fall, in careless and benighted hands, before the work of restoration began.

PROBLEMS OF DATING

Dating is another, intricate and involved, problem. Styles in the earlier times, up to and including the T'ang dynasty (618–906), must have been sensibly different from the general later range of Southern Sung (1127–1279), Yüan (1271–1368), Ming, and Ch'ing. Our chief guide to the culmination of the earlier period, much more remote from us than the later, is what has been almost miraculously preserved in the way of certain, for the greater part minor, pieces—stands for various objects, boxes, and other similar articles—in the Japanese treasure housed in the imperial repository known as the Shosoin in Nara. These are authentic seventh- and eighth-century importations to Japan, temple gifts and personal possessions, from T'ang dynasty China, hoarded through the centuries and now in themselves a further treasure of invaluable evidence by which we may in part reconstruct a vanished past.

They demonstrate to what heights of refinement a cosmopolitan and sophisticated court, enamoured of great luxury, had brought a whole range that had had its beginnings in the first millennium before our era, or even earlier. The extraordinary refinement and finish of all these T'ang pieces—made when European Christendom was still going through its Dark Ages—is remarkable.

In the tragic times that ushered in the end of this brilliant dynasty, and during the inroads of the barbarian Liao (907–1123) and Chin (1114–1234), the picture becomes more obscure. It is possible that in this very time of transition certain non-Chinese elements were added: one cannot as yet pronounce clearly on this point. The conquering Yüan rulers, being fundamentally of nomadic stock, seem also to have left no clear trace on furniture design. During their comparatively short period of overwhelming power we know that they borrowed on a grand scale, arranging grandiose installations in their new capital of Peking, somewhat at random apparently, and adapted to their own purposes. Yet the whole setting and the way of life it implied never came so close to them, as a people, as their tents and their carts, their portable possessions, in spite of the great attraction of Chinese civilization for such a dazzling ruler as Kublai Khan (1260–1294).

In the arrangement of his newly built, thirteenth-century Forbidden City itself, within a capital city also new, we know of the general quality of the rich installation from the vivid descriptions of Marco Polo and from certain Chinese sources as well. We even hear, for example, of woodwork of "fragrant" *tzu-t'an*, sought from abroad at great expense for buildings in the palace, one of which was even named the Purple Sandalwood Hall. Yet we have no detailed description of furniture proper; and except at court or at "Xanadu"—the upper capital, in Jehol—in the summer, felt yurts rather than permanent shelter were used by this nomadic people as a whole, as in Mongolia today, with rugs for their circular floors and apparently not much furniture beyond a few portable items.

With both the Northern and the Southern Sung dynasties (960–1126 and 1127–1279), and in the native culture of Central China, which in part preceded the Mongol period and culturally outlasted it, we are on much more familiar ground. Even if actual specimens are practically nonexistent, we have other evidence. We can, for instance, see a whole collection of various accessories used by Sung emperors and empresses in one familiar series of palace ancestor portraits; and these begin to show, quite clearly, for example, types of tables and chairs related to those in this book. Ming (1368–1644) and Ch'ing (1644–1911), which followed this rather than the Northern nomadic tradition, seem as of yesterday; and for these two prosperous dynasties we finally have the convincing evidence of a fairly large number of well-preserved objects.

Putting all that we know together, and with all the resources of modern critical scholarship to help us, it is nevertheless impossible, even from as late a time as the advent of the first Ming emperor in 1368, to construct any definite scale for dating of a kind familiar in the West; and it may remain impossible for several reasons.

The first reason, which is difficult for Westerners unfamiliar with the grand time-scale of Chinese history to grasp until they come to a comprehension of the ultimate meaning of this aspect of Chinese civilization, is that the great period of the first invention, the grand creation, lies embedded very far indeed in the past. We are dealing with a people that has had perhaps the longest unbroken record of social development in the world. When we have come far down extended ranges of time, therefore, to the point where actual examples, such as those illustrated in this book, begin to appear, a large number of the time-honored elements of Chinese design, in every branch of her arts, had already been in existence for an exceedingly long period.

The rate of change in making new adaptations from this repertory, moreover, had, in the age we are now concerned with, become comparatively slow. By this time the cabinet-maker had long possessed an extremely rich and familiar collection of elements, established and traditional, always at hand and convenient to draw from. Minor variations could easily be devised again and again; and so often was this done, as the fundamental designs to which they were added changed rather sluggishly, that it is extremely difficult—although not, perhaps, ultimately impossible—to construct a definite series of progressive points marking dated changes in style. It is quite impossible to do this in detail—phase by phase, at times almost decade by decade—as one often can, for example, in Gothic and Renaissance Europe.

As in Chinese painting, several varieties of archaistic return to the past, in different hands, might easily be in progress simultaneously. Only when much more work has been done on all this material may our vision be sharpened sufficiently to fix the definite time when certain pieces were made, by what the imitative designer or carver left, consciously or unconsciously, uniquely of his own period.

Finally, there were never the clear lines of demaraction to be traced to individual production which have existed so familiarly in Western Europe—in part because of its political and social system—that we have rather unreasonably often come to demand that they be found elsewhere. No family of great repute, like the Caffieri, and no artist like André Charles Boulle (1642–1732), who could himself and in his own person originate a fashion and then have posterity attach his name to it, ever existed in China.

Another fact that makes dating by stylistic analysis of ornament still very difficult in that the Chinese themselves have never paid much serious attention to it in any appraisal of their own furniture. Thus we have no secure documentation, either in careful drawings or even in detailed description, contemporary or of later compilation, to guide us. The Chinese spirit of investigation, their variety of curiosity, has in this field been very unlike ours; and if one asks quite different questions one naturally receives different answers. To learned Chinese trained in the old tradition, indeed, such material was simply not interesting enough, fine though it might be, to merit the prolonged scholarly contemplation considered fitting for such respected and well-cultivated fields, for example, as the history of the development of calligraphic styles or the design of old bronzes.

To be sure, by the mid-eighteenth century, in the *Dream of the Red Chamber,* we are given descriptions of elegant interiors, very much *à la mode,* elaborated with obvious satisfaction by the author of this novel, Ts'ao Chan (cir. 1715–1763), which make vivid to Chinese readers the setting of a powerful and ramified family at the height of worldly riches. Yet what category of chair was used for people of exceptional rank, where it was placed in a room, how small tables might be arranged for a family party (under the old system there could be no others among the womenfolk) —these matters interested the Chinese, and do to this day, far more than any attempt to classify such furniture chronologically or by categories of ornament, as we, in our much more time-conscious West, soon feel called upon to do. We therefore demand detailed information about matters never much noticed, and still less recorded once the present had slipped into the past, even by Chinese of both sensitiveness and erudition. Their minds were not turned in this direction.

Contemporary painting, too, which at first glance might promise to come to the rescue since its best testimony is the more accurate in that it is unconscious, becomes finally less useful than one might anticipate. For in the vast production of China, in a slight medium—thin color on paper or silk—that made enormous repetition and copying comparatively easy, styles in the delineation of furniture were so endlessly done over, with constant variation, improvised and elaborated according to changing fancy, that even if an interesting piece carefully represented in a dated scroll is found it is often impossible to determine how it came to be reproduced in that form, in that place.

The situation is somewhat the same as the portrayal of historic characters on the eighteenth-century stage in France and England before archaeological correctness had begun to be a concern of the modern mind. Except in a certain variety of genre painting of quite late date, as, for example, one famous series of illustrations for the very popular novel called the *Chin p'ing mei*,[2] the Chinese artist seems to have felt little compunction about improvising almost at random any given detail of costume and setting, even when "copying" a composition by some predecessor of reputation. No conscientious scruples impeded him, no stern desire for factual representation, and fantasy often beckoned to an individualist.

A certain number of unconscious details, some factual and quite highly technical, as for instance botanical varieties of woods—which we shall presently discuss—or details of joinery, may eventually help us to a moderate amount of valuable clarification. Indeed the marvelously skillful joints of the furniture in these plates, put together in every case with a minimum of glue, and with no nails under any circumstances, are in themselves almost a special field for study;

and here, to give different effects of profiling, there has been a definite development through time.

Also, unpretentious reproduction, such as woodcut illustrations in securely dated books, especially of contemporary scenes of the Ming and Ch'ing periods, may further permit us to form a helpful series of familiar pieces in common use at the time of their publication. The lack of self-consciousness of this last medium may be a safer guide toward veracity than the apparatus of formal painting—especially of historical scenes—with an understandable temptation to go searching for unusual and archaistic effects.

Further, with such a very long and rich past always accessible, in a vast country with a uniquely high level of aesthetic awareness and creative genius, a desire for ease and comfort and also individual pleasure seem often to have dictated the quality of private patronage. Then, too, if one installation could be made more elegant, or original, than another, whole changes in a familiar repertory of ornament would be rung in the attempt.

If we can suppose that the whole of Europe, under a single government, had never changed the main stream of its culture for some twenty centuries and that the greatness of a glorious and distant past, setting all aesthetic standards upon a broad and firm base, had been uninterruptedly revered generation after generation, we might possibly have had a variety of this same type of repetitive re-creation. When during the Renaissance in Italy, Catholic popes were accorded the honors and regalia of Roman emperors, there was a slight similarity of procedure.

Yet we can go, to a certain extent, beyond this. It is wise to remember that Chinese furniture was never an isolated phenomenon. It appeared and played its part in ministering to the arts of living along with the architecture, the carving in stone and wood, the textiles and the ceramics of its day. Gradual changes in all of these, fairly well determined for the Ming and Ch'ing periods, form the best possible ground against which to appraise the development of furniture. This always shared the tendencies of its age.

The evolution progresses, as seems the way in all human creation, from the simple toward the complex in any given phase, and from the early and functional to the late and highly ornamental. The plainer a piece illustrated in this book, the more likely it is to be Ming rather than Ch'ing, although one must also take into account fairly frequent, at times academic, "returns to the past." Until the frigidity of the late eighteenth and finally the decline of the nineteenth century sets in—here, as in all the other arts, also very obvious —we may not be able to assign pieces to the definite reign dates of great emperors as one might wish; yet the elaboration of Ch'ien-lung (1736–1795) is as obvious in a carved chair or table as in a porcelain vase or a piece of jade. There is also a progressive and important evolution of all underlying form, with the passage of time, in harmony with that of the other arts.

Some day, when we know more of wood, joinery, finish, and other technical details and have assembled perhaps a few dozen critical pieces, some of which—as occurs almost by accident—have been dated, we may more confidently move on to firmer ground. Meanwhile it is wise not to press conclusions. Early or late, strong or weak, functional or decorated—these qualities we can in many cases be certain about. Yet to draw an arbitrary line between late Ming and early Ch'ing production, for instance, especially from borderline specimens, in the present state of our knowledge would be imprudent and premature.

THE WOODS EMPLOYED

A further complication is that we can give no complete and comprehensive description of the exact variety of hardwoods—the modern scientific names—from which most of the examples of furniture illustrated in this book were made. At first glance this would seem a problem that today could certainly be solved with no undue difficulty, yet the situation is not a simple one.

China for so long has been deforesting herself, a process going on for many centuries throughout the whole of her habitable area, that the best of the cabinet woods here illustrated seem to have been procured, possibly even during Ming times, in large measure from beyond her borders. These are heavy, tropical woods, in some cases so dense in grain that they sink in water. Even as early as the great days of Kublai Khan (1260–1294), the Emperor had had *tzu-t'an,* or "purple sandalwood," imported for his palace halls; and the Philippines and the East Indies generally seem to have made their contribution quite regularly over the centuries to China's diminishing supplies.

Such wood, moreover, reached China in the form of cut logs so that, although a microscopic determination of the structure of the wood itself is easy enough with modern scientific knowledge, bud and blossom elude the botanist's search. He cannot pronounce definitely upon details of species, as opposed to the genus of the wood in general, until he has been able to inspect them, which with the old pieces, he now can never do. It is not as if one were dealing with trees common to European and American botany; these furniture woods come from different varieties in a part of the world where their complete history is often not accessible to us. We must therefore, provisionally, take what lead the Chinese give us, which sums itself up roughly as follows:

The best and most interesting pieces of furniture in this book are in general made of a wood called *hua-li,* which is very highly prized by Chinese connoisseurs. The local Peking furniture dealers distinguish several subvarieties of this: *lao hua-li,* old or dull *hua-li* (as well as *hsin hua-li,* or a newer variety) , besides the highly prized *huang,* or yellow, *hua-li,* which is a lighter shade of the best old wood.

This is probably what is known to botanists as *Pterocarpus indicus,* although others give it as *Dalbergia latifolia* or as *Ormosia henryi,* etc. Varieties are native not only to South China but also to such places as India, Burma, Sumatra, the Malay Archipelago, and the Philippine Islands. It is also known as Burmese or East Indian rosewood; and for a non-professional nomenclature rosewood seems a very good working name for it since in its lovely graining and delicate color it is not at all dissimilar to some of the many European rosewoods.

For those who have never seen examples it is difficult to convey the charm of the surface and color of fine old *hua-li.* A seeming translucence and satin-soft finish are perhaps its outstanding characteristics; and the blond varieties are often quite surprisingly light.

In the darker shades this wood has a cousin in the more common *hung-mu,* literally "red wood," much used for rather bourgeois, if expensive, pieces in the nineteenth century and in our own time. This seems to be of a related, though slightly inferior, family; and one can distinguish between two varieties; plain *hung-mu* and *lao,* old or dull, *hung-mu.* True *hua-li* is always brownish rather than reddish, and the best of it perhaps finer in grain than *hung-mu,* the finish of which is at times near to our mahogany.

One wood, however, is preferred even to *hua-li* by Chinese of the old school. This is *tzu-t'an,* literally purple sandalwood, the botanical name of which is said to be *Pterocarpus santalinus,* although it, too, is also attributed by some to the *Dalbergia* family. This wood is sometimes also called "blackwood," which seems a sensible working English equivalent since the wood is indeed often so dark as to be purplish in color. It is also perhaps the densest and heaviest of all the Chinese hardwoods, and it is this weight in particular that is respected by the Chinese dealer. Its dark color also gives it, in Chinese eyes, great dignity.

There is an esteemed subvariety of this wood for fine cabinetwork, not here represented, called by the Chinese *chin-ssu tzu-t'an,* or golden-threaded purple sandalwood. This is marked by slender fibers under the polished surface, which catch the light, like fine wires covered with foil, in such a way as to suggest its name. Such variants give the Chinese great pleasure.

Except for a certain quantity said to have come from Kwangsi Province, *tzu-t'an* seems native not to China but to Southern India, Annam, and the Philippines, etc., and hence to be a real importation. Its use is consequently indicative of the great labor not considered excessive to procure the finest possible materials for cabinetwork.

Much used for embellishing pieces often framed with these finest of the hardwoods, and therefore to be mentioned at this place, is *hua-mu,* or burl. In employing this material the Chinese take great and obvious delight in the natural curly patterns found when a good cross-section of root is exposed; and for inlay there is nothing they prefer to it, especially when both color and pattern are rich. In piece after piece in the accompanying plates, one may sense the pleasure with which it has been used.

Here is perhaps also the place, in our consideration of the best woods, to attempt to demolish the deep-rooted legend of "Chinese teak." Teak is an exclusively Indian wood, for Indian furniture. Modern, cheap treaty-port wares may perhaps occasionally have been made of inferior varieties of it, and "chop suey palaces" may occasionally be furnished with garish pieces actually of teak, yet it is not and apparently never has been a wood in traditional use for proper Chinese cabinetmaking. Ebony, or *wu-mu,* on the other hand, is occasionally found, especially for inlay work on pieces consciously elaborate.

After rosewood and blackwood, perhaps the next most prized variety for furniture of the best quality is a wood known as *chi-ch'ih-mu,* or "chicken-wing wood"; but it has a convenient—if somewhat inaccurate—working equivalent in English since it has also been called satinwood. There is no general agreement as to its botanical name; although *Cassia siamea* is apparently correct for one variety. This is not nearly so translucent as the woods already described, and it has a distinctly rougher grain and a much grayer and browner color. It is thus a less finished material than *hua-li;* but it is of enormous toughness and strength and is at its best for pieces not designed for the most formal effects. Excellent in durability, it is also a good working wood, and has rugged individuality. For Europeans a taste for Chinese satinwood may require a little cultivation; yet there are ranges of furniture for which it is extraordinarily well adapted.

After these, the finest, there follows a range of distinctly lesser woods; yet furniture made of them has by intention been included in this book to show a more comprehensive collection than merely that of pieces in the "noble" varieties just mentioned. One must rank *nan-mu*—which lacks a common English working equivalent—high among the secondary group. What is called *nan-mu* in China seems to be generally the *Machilus nanmu, Hemsl.* of the botanists. It is perhaps to be identified as a variety of cedar, although the best examples, when they take a glossy polish, are not altogether unlike walnut. While definitely below the woods already mentioned in quality, and above all without the wonderful translucence of *hua-li, nan-mu* is a useful wood for domestic pieces where a lighter tonality is desired. Its color shades off into yellow-browns and is at its best when used for simple or even slightly provincial design. A native of China, it is a durable, serviceable material.

We continue the list with another native wood represented in three varieties: *yü-mu; lao,* or old, *yü-mu;* and *nan,* or Southern, *yü-mu,* all of which are used primarily for sturdy, serviceable pieces. *Yü-mu* can be quite securely identified, as a genus, with our own elm.

Several other woods can also be given fairly secure definitions. There is *chang-mu,* or camphorwood, familiar and useful. For the Chinese as for us, it is a wood much prized in the making of good chests. Then there is *pai-mu,* corresponding to our cypress or cedar; and also a variety of pine—not a hard wood but used rather as deal—called *hsiang sha-mu,* or "fragrant pine." We have only one example of this in the present book; it is used as a cover for the ice chest, itself of finer material, in Plate 105.

Several less securely identified examples, bringing the total number of varieties and subvarieties here considered to about twenty, may close our list; no others are used for the furniture in these plates. There is *li-mu,* also *li-tzu-mu,* whether two terms for one wood, or quite possibly two different woods, I have not been able to determine without inspection of the pieces illustrated, now widely scattered. Several Chinese characters, which are all read *li* but in various "tones"—and therefore with the same sound may give quite different meanings—signify plum, which is unlikely, or pear (*Pyrus sinensis,* Ldl.) , or chestnut, a species of oak, or finally a chestnut-leaved oak (*Quercus serrata,* Thunbg., and *Quercus chinensis,* Bge.) . Now Chinese pearwood is occasionally used for making fine furniture; and cheaper pieces are also made of local chestnut, horse chestnut, or certain varieties of oak. This is a Chinese puzzle.

Finally, we have *ch'un-mu, huai-mu,* and *ch'iu-mu.* The first of these, *ch'un-mu,* is probably the *Cedrela sinensis,* Juss., a tree found in many parts of North, Central, and West China. It is a wood often used for good local furniture, and because of its aromatic odor is sometimes called, by Westerners, Chinese mahogany. *Huai-mu* can probably be identified with the *Sophora japonica,* L., which is one of the common timber trees of China, good for general construction and for furniture as well. It is used in only one plate in this book, No. 27, where it is combined, in a rather rustic little dresser, to form the top of a piece framed in elm, with drawers also of elm and panels of burl. To conclude, there is *ch'iu-mu,* used only in two places: for the sides of the tall wardrobe in Plate 3, which do not show in the photograph, and for Plate 5 where they are combined with the enigmatical *li-mu* for the top and bottom sections of a wardrobe in the traditional style. This has been identified as catalpa wood, perhaps either the *Catalpa Kaempferi,* S. and Z., or the *Catalpa Bungei,* C. A. Mey.[3]

HISTORICAL EVOLUTION

With the foregoing in mind, in this book we shall handle, category by category, actual types of household furniture in the only two dynasties from which the examples here illustrated can have come, Ming (1368–1644) and Ch'ing (1644–

1911). Yet from its origins hidden in China's ancient history, and over the long course of all the dynasties preceding these two—a span of several thousand years—Chinese furniture had developed and changed basically both in function and shape.

Here is not the place, nor is it the purpose of the present book, to discuss this evolution at any length. To do so would require an—as yet unwritten—historical monograph. Yet a few brief remarks may not be out of place. Two salient facts must be grasped by the Westerner at the outset. The Chinese historically had first lived low, on mats or platforms; as do the Japanese, who copied the earlier system, even to this day. Once the chair had been introduced, whence and when we do not as yet know in detail, and subsequently after its apparently irregular early appearance had finally gained general acceptance as a piece of furniture for daily use, it also brought with it a completely different set of desirables for living levels.

The furniture and domestic arrangements familiar in modern Japan still represent quite faithfully the T'ang and pre-T'ang system, for during the formative period of their history the Japanese had emulously adapted all things Chinese, taking over T'ang culture as completely as they could. As is well known, further, the Japanese still live habitually on the level of their floor mats, with no high tables and no chairs. This distinction between the use of the chair and the mat-covered platform for sitting is vital. It concerns the whole question of the level above the ground on which one proposes to live. The differences between the perspectives of the Forbidden City and of the palaces in Kyoto are examples of the end results. Many dissimilarities between Chinese and Japanese manners are also traceable to the wide gap between the two systems.

In North China, partly because of the general use of the built-in *k'ang,* both varieties and both levels were finally retained. This fact alone explains quite completely what otherwise might seem an anomaly in this book, for we shall see furniture that is both high and low, some suited to our habitual level and some not at all adapted, in its original intention, to it.

Now the Chinese of the Han dynasty (202 B.C.–A.D. 220) and their own ancestors originally had no chairs whatsoever; this is a firmly established and important fact. They habitually sat, or reclined, on flat surfaces much as the Japanese still do, sometimes with portable armrests, small stands to shift the weight of the body for comfort in this position. Chinese paintings, executed in archaistic style, often show the sages of antiquity either using mats spread upon the ground or seated in a variety of postures—often, also, with various types of low supports—upon low, broad wooden platforms which were generally covered with woven matting or some other material. In order not to soil the cover it was customary to remove all such footwear as had touched the earth before mounting the platform. This habit, later so universally adopted in Japan, was also maintained indoors and especially in early Chinese court ceremonial, where those granted audience removed their shoes before coming into the imperial presence.

This living-platform, for such it was, for use during the day, was of course closely related to the ancient Chinese bed, such as that depicted—higher and more like a modern piece of furniture—in a familiar scene in a fourth-century scroll attributed to Ku K'ai-chih or copied after him, in the British Museum, to which we shall revert later. Yet at this early stage the low platform should also be considered separately, since it was used for general purposes much as a flooring of mats is still used indoors in Japan. As a type of furniture it is therefore much older in style than any of the beds or couches illustrated in this volume; and although I know of no part of China where it still exists familiarly, large rectangular mats are today still commonly spread about—during the summer even in North China—when anyone wishes to sit or recline on the ground. The brick *k'ang*, of course, is this platform made permanent indoors.

Somewhere between the Later Han (25–220) and the T'ang dynasty (618–906) the chair first appeared, as early, it is said, as the middle of the second century of our era; it was perhaps used as a seat of honor, lay or secular, during the whole intervening period. This is the pivotal point in the whole development of later furniture styles in China, although as yet we are confined to speculation as to the detailed circumstances. In tracing the long and complex history, which it is hoped will one day be done, we lack actual objects to refer to for easy demonstration. One low bronze altar table, probably simulating wooden construction, a part of the Tuan Fang treasure in the Metropolitan Museum in New York City which is now generally accepted as of late Shang date or some time before 1000 B.C.; such materials as a replica of a model with detachable legs, in clay, probably of the Han dynasty;[4] some excellent T'ang examples of minor pieces of fine wood stored in the Shosoin at Nara, in Japan, and perhaps certain Yüan ones also in Japan; one—later—Sung chair and table: the number of pieces actually surviving from Chinese antiquity, even if this is only a summary enumeration of more or less familiar ones, is not great.

For later periods, painting and woodcut must of course be used but subject to certain gravely qualifying limitations already mentioned. At their best, though, these materials, especially for Sung and Yüan times, and also for the determination of Ming styles, may eventually yield us a rich harvest and help us construct a time-scale on which we can rely.

Finally, what the Chinese say about furniture proper in their own literature, which is on the whole sparse, needs codifying. The task has been begun by those modern Chinese who have incidentally gathered a few references to furniture in various compilations which serve as source books for Chinese economic history. There are surely many rich nuggets of this variety in unsuspected places yet to be unearthed. There exist, also, articles under the heading of furniture in the historic, large Chinese encyclopaedias, although these are on the whole not very informative. Cuts from one of them have been reproduced in this text.

In the present book, however, we shall merely examine those actual objects that have reached us in certain quantity and in usable condition, first discussing them briefly, category by category, in general as they appear in the plates that follow.

CUPBOARDS IN GENERAL

The cupboard with open shelves is ancient. One common Chinese character in current use, which is derived from a seal form here shown, is said to give a pictorial representation of it, including its shelves. This seal character probably dates from mid-Chou times. At what period doors were added, and hinges of various types first contrived and used, are as yet unsolved, perhaps even insolvable, problems. The whole scheme, though, must go back practically to the origins of carpentry, at least far into the Chou dynasty (1027–221 B.C.) or earlier. Here is another field for investigation.

There exist numerous examples of much later varieties in Sung and Ming painting, of course, and we illustrate one cut from a Ming illustrated primer now in the Library of Congress, in Washington, dated as of the early sixteenth century, that by this time gives an altogether familiar effect. The cut illustrates two models that 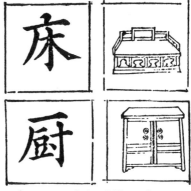 can be dated as of 1609. Thus, in general, by Ming times we are on solid ground.

Typical examples of glazed clay Ming tomb models, miniature in scale yet often carefully made, in the Brooklyn Museum collection, and others in the Royal Ontario Museum, the Buckingham Collection in the Art Institute of Chicago, and in the Chicago Museum of Natural History, etc., indicate with satisfying clearness all the detail of structure and framing in the ordinary Ming cupboard. It is noteworthy that in space division and paneling these popular types are definitely more complex than some of the elegant hardwood cupboards illustrated in this book, which were probably made for Ming and Ch'ing *raffinés* rather than in any sense furniture for the people. This more elaborate style, in softer and less precious woods, can often be seen in humble dwellings in North China, where it seems to have survived in the traditional production of local carpenters. The cupboard in Plate 6, with a tripartite division of its doors, approximates this variety more closely than any other example in this book; yet Plates 5 and 14 also belong to the same type.

WARDROBES

Of the whole family of wooden containers equipped with doors, the large standing wardrobe, or armoire, remains, even in modern times, the *pièce de résistance* of Chinese household furniture. Such wardrobes almost invariably come in pairs, often placed side by side or symmetrically along one wall, with perhaps a door in between, or opposite each other across a room. A complete set, as in Plate 1 (although this is of pieces photographed in the possession of a dealer, it has been reproduced here because it is complete), invariably consists of four pieces: two large cupboards, set on the floor, and on top of them a further pair of *ting kuei*, or "top cupboards," also called *mao kuei*, or "hat cupboards" because they were used to contain headwear above the clothing kept in the main pieces. When placed together, as in this plate, these constitute virtually the foundation of any Chinese installation; this is true—except for the throne itself—even in apartments of the Forbidden City, where examples reach mammoth size.

In the West, under contemporary conditions, we have now become so accustomed to dwelling in houses equipped with built-in closets that it is easy to forget how really modern they are. The typical heavy Victorian wardrobe, which dates from only yesterday, and the garderobes so commonly used all over the Continent remind us that unless special recesses were built into the walls this method of storing clothes in large pieces of movable furniture was once almost universal even in the West.

The use of the present-day coat hanger ought here to be considered. It would be interesting to trace its history, which is doubtless connected with the fashionable pressing of modern clothes. Chinese garments do not need this care; all of them have been for many centuries so fashioned that they could easily be folded into flat, rectangular piles, always ready for wear. The main creases were first vertical, the full length of the piece, and then horizontal; and if the fainter horizontal lines still showed a little when the garments were worn, they were symmetrical and neat, and even today are not considered in any way to detract from elegance. The coat hanger thus had no need to be invented in China.

Almost the only exception to this rule was the folding of such heavy garments as were made of or lined with fur. In order not to show seams exposing the pelt, these were usually given only vertical foldings if possible and laid away in *t'ang hsiang,* or "lying chests," generally of camphorwood. One example is given in Plate 101.

Historically, then, the wardrobe, and all the families of smaller cupboards that can be grouped about it, seems among the oldest of general types still in common use. One of its distinguishing features is the flush, vertical central bar or batten which is removable and which fits sidewise into projections in the framework, top and bottom. This bar is itself equipped with a pierced metal piece corresponding with two others, one on the frame of each door, the three in a horizontal row above the door pulls. This arrangement, given the broad and flat form of the ordinary Chinese padlock, with a skewer that can be threaded through all of them, keeps both doors securely and tightly closed. In Chinese cupboards arranged with two doors only, lacking this central member, there is a certain unavoidable play and the doors do not remain shut tight when locked. The Chinese, curiously enough, never seem to have devised inner catches to be set into the thickness of the door panels themselves, to fasten them securely to the frame. In the larger wardrobes this central batten is found invariably; and there as an integral part of the structure it adds to the general workability of the whole piece.

An additional detail to be noticed, especially in pairs of cupboards not meant to be used beside each other, is the batter or progressive diminution of their sides from bottom to top. This subtle lightening of proportions is one of the most pleasing refinements of many types of Chinese furniture. It is also commonly found in tables and chairs, in small pieces as well as large, and invariably imparts a singularly satisfying effect, making all forms pleasantly alive and springy. By the use of it, indeed, the Chinese handle inflexible wood in such masterly fashion that, almost unaware, one receives the impression of design in a living medium. Here is a feature that will repay serious and prolonged study by the modern craftsman, who is quite sure that he wants simplicity but whose productions, although today freed of much meaningless ornament, are all too often unfortunately "wooden."

SMALLER CUPBOARDS

In China it is characteristic that almost every design of every object in the endless repertory of native handicraft exists in many scales. Whole series of cupboards thus might be formed, ranging from huge palace examples, high as a small house, of superb wood and heroic carving, and capped at times by several tiers of upper cupboards, through models of half size, down to minature, as illustrated in a measure in this book. The original uses for some of the smaller and more individual of these should not be too arbitrarily designated now that they have traveled so far from their original owners. Quite apart from their obvious fitness to contain such objects for scholar-collectors as books and manuscripts or scroll paintings—rolled pictures in China, of course, take up relatively little space—those of precious woods must have been ideal for any small objects, for *bibelots,* such as snuff bottles, inkstones, or seals, or for the numerous other appurtenances of the writing table in which the Chinese take such particular pride and which they so enjoy possessing.

OPEN CUPBOARDS

The originality and variety of Chinese shelves is extraordinary; there is seemingly no end to their arrangement for special uses or for housing special objects nor any limit to the geometrical ingenuity by which these ends are accomplished. This is a characteristic already familiar to the instructed Westerner; in lacquer, even in pieces of inferior quality, similar shelves are common enough in the repertory of rather gaudy *chinoiserie;* they are also used prodigally in cheap objects from Japan. In finer design, however, they are more subtly contrived.

None of the open hardwood cupboards, as here illustrated in Plates 14 to 17, seems to have been made, however, as a single piece. Duality—such is the Chinese sense of the fitness of things—was often carried out even to the detail of the display of ornaments in a room. Pairs of vases or of flower pots, for example, were often an adornment for a side table, with always one single central piece, commonly called the *chu,* or "master" one, between the pair or pairs. Even if a seemingly impromptu asymmetrical arrangement was set out, as is so often seen in paintings, a second arrangement—similar although perhaps the full length of a room away—was often used to bring the first group into balance. Since the single cupboards here illustrated are themselves often asymmetrical, their opposites—like the two hands of a pair of gloves—must therefore generally be imagined to complete the furnishing of a room of any consequence in such a way as to satisfy Chinese eyes.

DRESSERS

The Western dresser or chiffonier with drawers for clothing, as used in a bed- or dressing-room, was so rare in China before the "foreigner" introduced the type in his own style and for his own use during the course of the nineteenth century as to be practically nonexistent. Even today it shows no sign whatsoever of being adopted as a Chinese piece. The reason for this is partly due, as one will have anticipated, to the form of native clothing worn by both men and women; yet it is also true that the Chinese stow in chests what we should normally lay away in drawers and that they prefer to put under lock and key much of their clothing that is not in immediate use. In this they are apparently not unlike most peoples of medieval and some of modern Europe.

In temples, nevertheless, to hold various paraphernalia for ceremonies and sacrifice or to use in front of an altar, but also in domestic use—especially in rooms for eating where it was convenient to store crockery and other utensils—the dresser with one tier of drawers only, rather than with several in depth, has long been familiar. It must be remembered that in China, in the older tradition, there was almost never a single room in a house set apart for dining purposes only. Thus the buffet or sideboard never attained the elaboration and formal development it reached—with table manners—

for example, in England. Eating, for the typical Chinese even today, proceeds according to curiously intimate and personal desires as to time and place.

Of course adaptations to special circumstances were made. Besides the unpretentious and familiar *lien san,* or "three-in-a-row," used to hold eating utensils, with its three drawers above and generous storage space below, one may also find, as here illustrated, a number of other pieces with drawers that have obviously been made for carefully planned settings. Often these also have quite capacious cupboards at the bottom, below drawer level; but it should be mentioned that in Chinese eyes an arrangement for blind storage—without cupboards—was also a simple and convenient domestic makeshift, especially in a land where numerous growing children were eternally present in the family circle. Access to the well below the drawers was simply had by taking out the drawers and groping about in the space below, an arrangement apparently not considered undignified in daily living.

A word about the drawer itself. It exists, familiarly in China as in the West, with drawer pulls or bails, and even with inset locks, although more normally with metal lock shields and projecting loops to accommodate the conventional, and detachable, Chinese padlock. It seldom fits as accurately and tightly into its framework, however, as does our own drawer. Perhaps the Chinese never really ceased to regard it merely as a *ch'ou t'i,* or "pullable tray," which remains the common term for it. The Japanese and the Koreans, of course, also use drawers; all these related peoples are much aware of the amenity of putting objects away separately and by categories. Extremely large and deep paper-lined trays, indeed, are said to have been used by palace eunuchs, as recently as in the years of the last Empress

Dowager, to keep together various parts of her many costumes.

Chinese trays of various depths, too, often come fitted together in a number of superposed layers, as in covered food boxes or picnic baskets, to serve as separate partitions for some common purpose. If these were to be encased in an enveloping framework, and each provided with its separate pull, they would become proper tiers of drawers in a modern chest; and for apothecaries' wares, for instance, this type of cupboard does exist familiarly. Many smaller pieces, such as dressing cases, are also fitted with superposed drawers, often of different sizes. Yet for household use, for intimate clothing and personal possessions, all through the centuries the larger multitiered dresser never seems to have suggested itself generally to Chinese taste. Perhaps the familiar use of many small boxes instead made the capacious cupboard below drawer level, which is the alternative, indispensable.

TABLES

Until the chair gained general acceptance in China, the small low table alone seems to have been the familiar type, and this, as we have seen, is a form of great antiquity. We have already mentioned one example, of what is probably an imitation of wooden construction, in the celebrated bronze altar table from the Tuan Fang treasure in the Metropolitan Museum. This is not equipped with legs but is made up of what are apparently simulated, pierced, panels set within a rectangular framework enclosed horizontally both top and bottom. The Han dynasty clay model already mentioned, however, does have true legs, curiously enough in the form of a beast's, with hoofs. No early example with legs like our own modern type has ever, to the best of my knowledge, been found.

The change in level, necessary if the domestic table was to serve all purposes required of it by people seated in chairs, gradually led to the development of types familiar to us in the West; yet it is to be noted that the *k'ang* tables in this book, at proper height only when used from the other and older, cross-legged level, still echo at times quite faithfully what must have been the earlier arrangements.

By the Sung period we have one actual example of a proper table. In effect it is much like the true table in other lands with a squared top, four legs, and some system of bracing to make them better able to withstand use. This is a companion piece to a chair we shall presently discuss.

One of the chief uses of the table, of course, was for eating. The absence of a round table in this book is a real lack, since Chinese family eating habits often favored its use in a familiar size, the radius of which could not be greater than the length of the human arm. Dishes placed in the center could thus be reached by all those seated about it, using chopsticks to take their food from large common bowls. This intimacy and comfort the Chinese find so natural, in their own system, that even a large dinner party in the traditional Peking of yesterday was never prepared for by any of the arrangements of combined boards familiar for banqueting in the West; the arrangement was nearly always of multiples of so many single "tables," usually round and arranged to seat only from ten to twelve persons.

There is, however, a common variety of square dinner table much used for feasting, and frequently rented out by caterers, often in bright lacquer or in plain varnished wood. This is commonly seen at the staple festivities of Chinese life, at weddings, birthdays, or funerals, and is called the *Pa*

Hsien cho, or "Eight Immortal table." Several examples of a slightly smaller variety but made on the same principle are illustrated in this book.

In traditional celebrations, in the houses of the wealthy, tables were also used at private theatrical performances, when the guests were invited not only for a series of plays but also for feasting and drinking tea or rice wine during them. Yet even here, opposite a stage, the arrangement was always one of tables that were arranged for small and intimate groups.

Stools, also, rather than chairs were invariable for dining, except when special honor was to be shown to one person—as at a sixtieth birthday feast for a parent, for example, which in the old China always called for a very special and elaborate celebration. Older persons, though, as we shall see, could use chairs generally. Otherwise, stools were placed symmetrically about any dining table; and although not specially comfortable for Westerners, they never seem to be considered inadequate by old-fashioned Chinese.

SMALL TABLES

The small table is in China, as in most countries, a common piece. Yet in China it was often felt to be too bare merely by itself; and historically it was commonly enriched by the use of an "apron" of some fabric, perhaps even with a flounce and streamers, as is so often seen in pictures. The frontality of this arrangement, for the apron was frequently used only on the face opposite the spectator, or at most around three sides, is testimony of how much emphasis the Chinese set on the position from which a piece of furniture is to be seen. From this side it exists; from other angles its detail is often disregarded. At funerals these aprons are still commonly fastened to tables in the temporarily erected *ch'a p'êng,* or "tea sheds," when groups of friends or associates wish to show politeness by a ceremonial offering of tea to refresh the formal mourners as they walk with their paper-decorated wands in the procession behind the catafalque. This is formal dress for the table, corresponding to similar arrangements, as we shall see, for the chair.

WRITING TABLES

In general, since writing and painting are parts of a single art in China, there are very few desks, in the European sense of the word. Painting was often done upon a large flat table, merely called a *hua cho,* or "painting table"; and writing could be carried on similarly, wherever it seemed convenient to spread the numerous traditional materials—brushes, ink-stick, grinder, water, brush holder, wrist-rest, seals, ink-pad, etc. Nevertheless, there are certain pieces of furniture that seem to have been made as writing tables exclusively; and six of these are here reproduced since they are of special interest to Western designers.

SIDE TABLES

Walls in China are very often treated much as façades, requiring a permanent, flat, space-filling decoration. This was the more natural in that such an arrangement did not impinge upon the usually uncarpeted floor space which was to be left free for such use as might be required of it on formal occasions. This explains the general elongation and lack of breath of many of the pieces made for installation against a wall that are illustrated in this book. In modern living in the West, although our intention in obtaining uncluttered floor space is not at all the same as in the old formalistic China, this is nevertheless a valuable principle to consider.

One variety of Chinese side table is typical of that country alone, at least in its general design and ornamentation. This is the large, narrow and long, variety, or *t'iao-an,* which when its ends were curved upward, as was often done with pieces in the traditional style, is called a *ch'iao-t'ou,* or "upturned head" side table. This is a detail that in general makes a piece more formal. Smaller and lighter side tables using this same general scheme are also commonly called *an-tzu.*

These, however, are usually flat. The *t'iao-an* has, as a rule, a fairly narrow top in proportion to its length; but it is also generally supported, not on legs, but by a framework set near each end into which panels of carving, often of rich openwork design, are commonly set. All the strength of strong construction, the delicacy of good profiling, and the refinements of splay are lavished upon these supports; and the often quite elaborate carving within seems to have followed fashion more regularly than the detail of almost any other type of furniture. Perhaps these openwork panels, if systematically analyzed, will one day serve as a helpful criterion for better dating, especially since in their design they are more closely connected with the other arts.

The *t'iao-an,* it may thus be seen, has no exact analogy with any piece of European furniture. Since it was long and was usually placed on axis in the center of its wall, it tends also to formality and height, so that the larger examples are often considerably higher than Western side tables even when the latter are also formal pieces of furniture. It is above all that piece, in the range of Chinese tables, in which strict frontality and symmetry are consciously emphasized.

ALTAR TABLES

A few words ought also to be said about the altar table, although it is not—unless used in a family shrine—strictly a domestic piece. Those for temples, which often were very large and unwieldly, and of great bulk, were planned as monumental surfaces to receive formal rows of altar furniture, the usual "sets of five"—candlesticks, flower vases, and an incense urn in the center—or the baskets and various containers for the victuals used in formal sacrifice. Often of rich red lacquer and heavily ornamented in gold, they represented conservative, completely traditional types of design; they are thus in interesting contrast with much lighter and slenderer pieces for household use. In both material and decoration they are the very opposite of the delicate *hua-li* furniture shown in these plates. Yet one example in excellent hardwood has been included here: the elegant small table—probably made for some private ancestor hall—shown in Plates 23 and 24.

LUTE TABLES, ETC.

Also to be mentioned are lute tables, especially proportioned to hold a Chinese zither; semicircular ones; nests of them, very popular in China-trade wares and in Japan; and odd small shapes in general. The Chinese here have taken obvious pleasure in displaying ingenuity in work on a lighter and more delicate scale. For garden pavilions there is literally no end to the varieties devised. The lute table, however, was always restrained to a certain dignity; the Chinese have had far too great a sentimental affection for this instrument through the centuries not to have expended special care on every appurtenance connected with it.

Later, a word or two will be said about the familiar, low *k'ang* tables, six of which are illustrated. Historically, it has been seen, these probably go back to a remoter past than any of the other varieties mentioned, and their design invariably shows it. They must always be appraised, however, with their height for a seated person in mind; only then do their best points count at their full value.

THE BUILT-IN *K'ANG*

We shall now discuss the permanent, as opposed to the movable, *k'ang*, which must precede any treatment of the wooden bed since in North China the *k'ang* is a part of the actual construction of the house, and as such probably dates from a very remote period. Although it is not, strictly speaking, a piece of furniture, no discussion of Chinese interiors could pretend to completeness without preliminary consideration of this felt- or mat-covered platform; indeed in much of the interior of North China country people know of no other way to sleep, and they spend hours of each day upon it as well. It is slightly lower than average seat height, both in the town and country, and usually runs, in ordinary houses, completely across one side of nearly all rooms used for common living. It is also in general of a depth comfortable to recline on. Almost invariably faced with slabs of gray building brick and often given some decorative touch of minor carving, the *k'ang* is nearly always mildly heated for winter use by interior flues which carry warm air under its brick surface from a soure of heat placed within, or without, the walls to the room of which it is a part.

Palace examples, being grander than others, often had large pits excavated under the eaves of an outside porch to take care of the fire making, and during the summer these were ordinarily covered over with fitted wooden planking. Yet in poorer houses a small and simple "fire cart," an iron frame on wheels equipped with a diminutive asbestos stove to hold glowing balls, made of coal dust mixed with earth or clay, would be pushed into a narrow tunnellike aperture in the floor, where it would slowly give off heat and thus warm the upper surface through flues arranged with exterior vents. Or a small open fire could be built in a sunken ovenlike depression under the inner wall of the *k'ang* itself, which could be stoked conveniently from within the room.

It is on the brick *k'ang* that humble families still spend much of their time; here they remove their shoes or slippers before mounting, and wear only the typical Chinese cloth socks, generally blue and stitched like a short, loose boot, with quilted soles of clean white cloth. To have these socks clean was always a point of pride to people of respectability in the old tradition. Here the men smoke or drink tea, while the women sew or busy themselves with other domestic tasks; here the North Chinese feel that one can be truly comfortable.

Among the lower classes it can fairly be said that the *k'ang* is the center of the life of the household; although even in splendid apartments within the Forbidden City itself, it was a permanent part of the North Chinese interior. It possessed its own furniture which—in contrast to all that we have already discussed—is distinctly low, since it is used by people immobilized in sitting posture. It is therefore often more like pieces familiar in Japan than any other category in China. The historical developmnet, as we have seen, explains the initial resemblances; Japan, having copied T'ang models, then retained them so completely, adding no others, and so adjusted her national life for about a thousand years to this lower level, that a Japanese house may be said in one sense to be all *k'ang.* Any traveler in Japan who, at the entrance to some local inn, has removed his Western shoes, muddied from the streets, while sitting on the high benchlike step in the doorway before rising in stocking feet to mat level, will comprehend this.

In North China, however, perhaps as one result of repeated historic invasions from the North and West, whence another system may early have been imported, both levels and both varieties of furniture heights were finally retained and used together; thus—as in this book—we can observe two fundamentally different groups mingled. One harmonizes well, except for minor differenecs of proportionate height, with our own system of tables and chairs; the other is a variety with which the ordinary Japanese would feel more familiar—a platformlike living surface at squatting or kneeling level.

K'ANG FURNITURE

Most typical of all its furniture, the Chinese *k'ang* is generally provided with its own low central table, which can be used by those seated tentatively along its edge, out of politeness, as well as by the ranking members of the household who once—somewhat more frequently than today, one gathers—installed themselves cross-legged upon it. This table is often made of excellent wood since it is a much-used piece of furniture in which house owners take obvious pride. A guest is often served tea upon it, these days in general merely seated with his host, one at each side of the table.

Good examples of *k'ang* tables brought from China also serve us, by happy chance, for the popular coffee tables, at present much in use in the West; yet the original place for these was never on the floor, as the uninitiated almost invariably assume, but on the higher level of the *k'ang*. Here they are seen as they were meant to be.

Besides this table, however, on the *k'ang* were generally placed other low pieces of furniture, on some of which it was customary to pile folded quilts during the day. For it must be remembered that, in cold weather especially, the heated *k'ang* was the normal sleeping place for everyone, while the rest of the house, except for very occasional braziers or portable foot warmers, might remain frigid. Since it was also in use during the day, some place had thus to be devised for the bedding which, when of quilted silk or even merely wadded cotton, was in simple homes often a proud possession, and to be displayed. Low pieces, such as those in Plates 66 and 67, were considered fitting—in a domestic setting—for this purpose.

The *k'ang* cupboard, large or small, rich or plain, was always quite low. It was usually set against one of the side walls to complete the furnishing, and pairs were quite general. None of these is ever very deep, and on the whole they do not take up much room. Their drawers and cupboards were used chiefly as receptacles for possessions to be used on the *k'ang* itself.

Complete the traditional installation of this Chinese dais with rich rugs of deep pile in glowing colors, for this was above all the place for which many of them were woven, and also with carpeted or embroidered flat, rectangular cushions and generously stuffed back rests; arrange it so that cups of hot tea can always be at hand, with ingenious hollow cup-rests to prevent staining the furniture; and the *k'ang* becomes what it represents to millions of average North Chinese: that place in his whole house where he can most pleasantly install himself; the corner where he can gossip and feel wholly at his ease. It is thus not surprising that some of the most attractive pieces represented in this book were obviously made for use on the *k'ang*.

THE BED

As early as the Later Han dynasty (25–220), we have references to "dust-catching" canopies above the bed-platforms of that time and also to the elegant arrangement, with curtaining, of such private alcoves. This continues down the centuries. We know, for example, of Yüan sleeping arrangements with very elegant curtains and elaborately decorated screens. From such details it is easy to see how the richly ornamented private sleeping place gradually evolved, and from it finally the movable canopied bed of hardwood which, as in Plate 40—except for its low railing opening in the middle of one side only instead of along both sides as with us— had developed by Ming and Ch'ing times to become not unlike a contemporary European bedstead.

As early as in the scroll already mentioned of the "Admonitions of the Instructress to the Ladies of the Court" either by Ku K'ai-chih, who lived about 344–406, or else copied after him, we have a delineation of what is a true bed, curtains, screening, and footstool complete. A word must be said, however, about the arrangement of the bedding. Upper and lower quilts were usually not kept spread over the bed during the day, as in the West, but were folded in a series of shallow, lengthwise pleats and set at the back along the wall. A pad, in pictures often represented as bordered in some flowered material, was commonly used in their place like a single thin mattress; and the bed then formed a hard sitting surface.

Pillows, as is familiarly known, were also hard, and through the centuries every possible material was used. Some were of porcelain, to be filled with hot water in winter or ice in summer; but varieties in flexible strips of polished bamboo or of lacquered leather, or also of finely woven rattan, hollow and stretched on a framework, were common. Peasants and unpretentious people, even today, in the North generally use dark blue cloth with a stuffing of various kinds of chaff and a shape square in cross section. Even collapsible pillows of jointed wood exist for the wayfarer. All of them, however, are to give fairly high, firm support to the nape of the neck rather than to cushion the head.

In South China the canopied wooden bed seems at times to have reached extreme elaboration, being equipped, in numerous examples, with a separate, roofed "antechamber" attached at the level of its flooring and wide enough to accommodate small pieces of furniture at each end. The whole of such a structure might be raised a step or so higher than the ground so that when its curtains were drawn it formed a completely isolated sleeping unit, equipped with all necessaries, not altogether unlike a modern railway compartment. In a land of many servants and in the large families of China, where it has been said that a locked door is often regarded domestically as a social offense, this room within a room did give some measure of privacy.

THE STOOL

The universal use of the stool in China requires a certain amount of explanation, in part also historic. In the dwellings of the poor, and even much further up in the economic scale, stools still comprise by far the greater number of all pieces used for sitting. We have seen that even in houses of wealth, stools alone, even today, are placed about the table for dining both in the family circle and for guests. Their use is invariable in eating houses or restaurants, or when the ever present caterer supplies the furniture for one of the larger ceremonies in Chinese life, such as a wedding or a funeral, where even the poor invite great numbers of—politely contributing

—guests. To ask a person, in a traditional Chinese setting, to dine with you from a chair is thus to do him special honor; and Ming woodcut illustrations show this clearly. It was, however, one of the major politenesses shown to the aged; they are very often, if really old, shown in pictures as dining seated in chairs.

It appears possible that as civilization progressed in China, men sat ever farther away from the ground; first directly upon it, no doubt, then later upon mats, as we can see in familiar arrangements in paintings where the sages of old are represented. Those of rank were placed upon low, broad wooden platforms, also provided with matting, and these seem gradually to have developed until they finally became true couches, Many later pictures show examples of them being used by personages of honor, while next to them sit secondary figures in armchairs, themselves attended by still others a little lower on stools.

The conservative tendencies of religion should also be mentioned. Priests, quite frequently even today, sit cross-legged; they often have about them, in Buddhist temples or Taoist halls, older, lower, and broader types of furniture —consciously archaic—that are more convenient for this variety of sitting posture. To them, this is a part of the dignity of their station.

Servants, and the lower classes generally, still hold to old customs. In recent times in North China it was still a familiar sight to see them half squatting on very cheap, extremely low, diminutive stools of unpainted wood, which they could buy from itinerant vendors, when resting from work in warm weather in the courtyard or at the doorstep. Only lithe Chinese bodies seem flexible enough to be quite comfortable on so exiguous and so low a support. The small square stools, usually of varnished soft wood, commonly found today in almost every ordinary Chinese household for hard wear and use, are also somewhat lower than the ampler ones of precious woods illustrated in this book.

Historically, the stool in all its varieties is a familiar and much-used piece of furniture. Curiously, it is one of the few that were quite normally given a certain amount of upholstery in earlier days, cushions being fastened to it by means of cords, often passed through apertures in the framework, and tasseled. Circular stools, or barrel seats, in both painting and woodcut, show this arrangement more often than not. It is said that in T'ang times a stool was considered the ideal seat for a woman, displaying as it did the curve of her back, her neck, and her shoulders to best advantage, while yet it was considered modest for her so to seat herself.

One transitional type should be mentioned; a stool provided with a low back rest, the ends of which tend to be extended so as to form true arms. Examination of old paintings will uncover many examples. This may have been one of the ways in which the Chinese chair came spontaneously into being; or it may be that it is merely a proof of the far-reaching influence of the chair.

THE CHAIR[5]

It is in the use of the chair that the Chinese approach us

 in the West more closely than any other Asiatic people. All men recline for rest, and most must walk about upon their errands in this world. Yet how they sit, during ceremonies, while eating, or in their hours of labor and leisure, is what distinguishes them from their neighbors; and this distinction we feel deeply somehow to be fundamental.

We have touched briefly on the major problem of where the chair came from: perhaps from the South and India, with Buddhism and all the paraphernalia of Indian culture that arrived in its train, or perhaps transmitted from the North by other Asiatic peoples, possibly even all the way across Asia and ultimately from the classical world. The answer, or answers, to a problem which may have several, as yet we do not definitely know. Traces of the record are swallowed up in Chinese antiquity and it is of course quite possible that all sources may have played their part in the final evolution. We are commonly told that the chair appeared not earlier than the middle of the second century of our era; and we have one and perhaps the earliest known representation of it in a carved stele in the William Rockhill Nelson Gallery of Art, in Kansas City, which can definitely be dated as of 535–540. An important clue that a variety of it was in fact a Northern importation is its common early name of *hu ch'uang,* or "barbarian couch."

The author has in his possession a small photograph of an actual Sung example from an excavated tomb, which was found together with the table already mentioned; it is completely modern in general lines, although it is, understandably enough, in a battered condition. This is said to have been found in Chü-lu hsien, in southern Chihli, a village overwhelmed when the Yellow River suddenly changed its course in the year 1108. It was once known to the authorities of the Historical Museum over the Wu Mên, or main gate, of the Forbidden City in Peking, and was said a decade ago to be in a minor museum, if memory serves, in Tientsin, but what has become of it during the long years of the last war is uncertain.

As for the practical shape of Ming and Ch'ing examples, one must begin with one initial consideration before pronouncing on general questions of comfort. Although not so small in stature as the Japanese, the Chinese in general—although by no means always—have smaller bodies than modern Westerners. It also ought not to be forgotten that the eighteenth-century European was by no means so tall as his well-nourished descendants of today.[6] Now the ordinary chair, in any country, has this particularity that more than any other piece of furniture it must be fitted, if it is to be comfortable, to the proportions of the user. With this in mind, it will become clear that many Chinese chairs are really adjusted with extreme nicety, and that not only their general size but also their structure adapts them, in detail and often with a high degree of refinement, to the normal seated figure.

Chinese chairs, too, exhibit diversity both of material and of fittings. One can progress all the way from upholstered cushions upon large wing chairs for winter use, through cooler bamboo and rattan, to chairs with light openwork frames and marble seats and backs, usually far too squarish for the Westerner, yet traditionally considered suitable for use in summer. The Chinese is acutely conscious of the tactile quality of the surface he sits on and will go to no little trouble to have his furniture proper for the season. One might mention that it was considered quite impolite in the old days to offer a Chinese a chair that had recently been used by another.

There is also a whole hierarchy of specified uses. The use of an armchair, or *fauteuil,* as opposed to a chair not provided with arms, the simple *chaise,* was under the old order as in the old Europe definitely a prerogative of rank. Stools, as we have seen, and barrel seats, were still lower in the scale. It should also be said that for personages of consequence merely thus to be given an armchair was not enough. Furs or rich stuffs had first to be thrown over it so as almost completely to cover the framework. Tiger skins—the rule for military officials generally—were especially honorable, but brocade or brocade-bordered silken fabrics were also commonly used. Careful inspection of many varieties of Chinese painting, from conventional ancestor portraits, using folding chairs which were the seats of ceremony for this purpose, to genre scenes of every description, will show these throw-overs as in very common use. Except on the theatrical stage where the whole scheme is still retained, they have been almost completely abandoned in contemporary life. Even so, in the Peking of yesterday, at ceremonies in temples, or for festivities such as birthday parties in the special halls for such purposes in certain restaurants, a shabby chair was still occasionally given this decoration.

In the plates here reproduced, attention has been concentrated chiefly on armchairs with round or square backs and a few varieties of simple light chairs without arms. Yet there are a number of other ranges. Traveling chairs, collapsible, form one important family, here omitted as being relatively less important for ordinary household use, at least in modern times. Their careful reproduction in countless ancestor portraits, however, shows the esteem in which the Chinese commonly held them. They were apparently an essential for the journeys of court officials, and above all for the Emperor himself—at all times out of doors, with screening of one variety or another behind them.

Then there are easy and reclining chairs of a great many varieties. Many of these have a curious polelike horizontal projection for each arm over which the sitter could throw his leg. It is to be remarked that the Chinese very easily place their legs high, often putting the sole of one foot upon the seat of a bench or chair, for comfort, while the other leg hangs to the ground in a manner not natural for Westerners. The easy chair, with a movable headrest and an extension to pull out for reclining, is pleasantly known as a

tsui wêng i, or a "drunken lord's chair." An example—portraying a scene of complete domestic comfort as of 1681— is shown herewith.

VARIOUS CHESTS, BOXES, ETC.

The Chinese way of life, involving large family groups, numbers of servants, and little privacy, is reflected in the use of a large variety of chests of every conceivable size and material which, when it was considered necessary, could generally be securely locked. The design of these chests is familiar; hinged at the back, they invariably have a pair of handles at the sides and also a typical lock shield and hasp, for a Chinese padlock, at the front. The sizes of these boxes go, as usual, from the mammoth to the miniature.

Illustrated in this book since it is of wood and in this case most suitably camphorwood, is a chest for furs—which could be folded to be put into it with perhaps only one horizontal crease—that is a little more than four feet long, although showy examples in the Forbidden City were often much larger in every way. Many chests were also made, traditionally, of lacquered or painted red leather, cheerfully decorated with a wealth of red or gold cut-out ornament. The liberal use of these confers, even today, a bright and typical note to Chinese interiors; and one must always picture the pieces of brilliantly polished hardwood furniture illustrated in this book with, somewhere in the scene, generous opaque Chinese red as a foil for their polish and fine translucence.

The ordinary Chinese family stores the clothing of other seasons, and indeed any objects not at the moment required, in many such chests, usually kept stacked and never far from sight. Although today we ourselves often buy European or Early American chests for their picturesqueness, we have in general forgotten how very useful such capacious containers can be, providing on the top of their storage space a horizontal surface of convenient area. More frequent use of them—for seldom-used objects—might prove practical in many places where today we unthinkingly set a small table, thus wasting the space beneath it.

TRADITIONAL DESIGN

One last remark on design. We have in this book dealt almost exclusively with a type of furniture conceived in an aesthetic highly adaptable to modern uses. It would not be historically correct, however, to leave unmentioned another type, also quite common, usually enriched with elaborate flangings and "fins" of ornament—occasionally reminiscent even of bronze styles. A few pieces illustrated come close to this style. That it is an ancient one may safely be inferred merely from the fact that much of the heavy red-and-gold altar furniture, sacrificial tables, shrine casings, etc., in some of the oldest and grandest temples in China, such as those to Confucius both in Ch'ü-fu and in Peking, is invariably in this style.

In much comparatively inexpensive traditional furniture, where a robust effect is desired, it is this style which is commonly used with a delightful repertory of freely executed conventional ornament. We also see not a little of it in old paintings. It would seem as if here was a whole range, never wholly abandoned in conservative or provincial work, where the local wood carver made use of his native skill. Some of it is very much like French furniture from the provinces and also, like this, is honestly done in local woods. It is quite possible that, in contrast with such a type, many of the pieces illustrated in this book represent a refined and rather scholarly taste, with special catering to personal preferences, and are thus almost an offshoot from the coarser, and more traditional, main stream of Chinese design. This forthright, cheerful, more elaborate variety of furniture—in humbler materials—needs to be collected, and analyzed, separately.

FURNITURE ARRANGEMENT

Several general matters, finally, also need mention: the proper arrangement of Chinese furniture, especially in a reception room, and also some detail concerning the height from the floor of the whole range of these pieces.

To a Chinese it is second nature to consider that the farther away from the entrance and the farther into a room one is invited, the more honorable the position conferred. So to "sit higher" in China is always an invitation to progress away from the drafts and inconveniences at the door. A throne, on axis, opposite it and against the north rear wall—formally oriented Chinese buildings invariably have their main entrance on axis, in the south wall of one of the long sides—was of course the most honorable seat of all. The Chinese is never unaware of the amenity of facing the sun, which in the grand scheme of things, should be squarely opposite the seat of honor at midday.

Secondary chairs, quite often although not always without arms, were generally placed with a small table between each pair, forming formal groups of three, flat against the rear or side walls. Often these were designed as a single unit. Here, too, there are further distinctions; those chairs on the host's left, the spectator's right, and therefore generally to the east, were always more honorable in Ming and Ch'ing times than a corresponding pair across the room and to the west. Nothing was left to chance. Nor was furniture ever placed in the center of an apartment in informal grouping. Indeed, the casual arrangement of modern Western furniture, especially with pieces not at right angles to each other, or not parallel to the walls of a room, is abhorrent even today to any Chinese schooled in the old tradition. Furniture groupings that are not balanced, or oblique, are to him simply uncouth.

As to the height from the floor, it must not be forgotten that, especially in North China, with ordinary construction of brick and no special arrangements for insulation against moisture from the ground and with floors almost always, even in palaces, of polished brick slabs, it was more comfortable, especially in cold weather, to keep feet up and away from the damp. This was the more so in that, except perhaps in a palace, floors were almost never covered with rugs or carpets; the variety of large, square, hard-baked gray brick (much prized for this purpose) that made the flooring was merely saturated with *t'ung* oil and then given so much rubbing that it finally had a gloss almost as of ebony. This was the familiar North Chinese floor in a house of quality—never parquet as with us.

So nearly all the chairs here illustrated have a front stretcher designed to serve as a footrest; and this, even though other proportions of the chair are slightly smaller than for Westerners, often brings the height of the seat a trifle above what is now normal with us. Even if no special rest is provided, it was once quite customary to use shallow, hardwood footstools. Chairs were made to be drawn up to tables, of course, thus further affecting the customary height of the table which, in general, is also a little higher than in the West. An exception is the ordinary dining table with stools, for, as we have seen, informal varieties of the latter are comparatively low, and the table that goes with them is therefore often in proportion, especially in humble settings.

CONCLUSIONS

From this review we can now proceed to certain conclusions. Yet, to make our picture complete, one further task of some magnitude and importance must be done. It is to be hoped that some day the architectural settings in which all

these individual pieces were placed can be studied in sufficient detail, with liberal documentation of earlier painting
to support conclusions, to determine and make clear the
many varieties of the traditional setting. This task does not
present insuperable difficulties for the Ch'ing dynasty, from
which many of the pieces here illustrated have come; and
fortunately we still have for this period quite enough left of
the actual settings themselves, although often badly deteri-
orated, to put the picture together successfully, if delays are
not excessive. One may then be able to work backward from
the familiar toward its origins.[7]

The final result will only confirm what the reader must
by this time have been able to gather for himself: the Chinese
have here created for themselves a whole world of design
with a complete aesthetic of its own. Component parts fit
perfectly into the general scheme; from large to small all is
calculated to produce an unmarred effect of dignity and balance. It is a world of polished hardwood, of superb quality,
in which every natural feature of the material has been skillfully handled so as to yield its best results. The same unity
pervades the design for interiors that once made so impres-
sive and satisfying the external aspect, the roofs and courtyards, of a great, regular, planned city of the size of Peking,
where all was unbroken harmony on a scale and with a completeness that must have had few parallels in the history of
the world.

We are not dealing with an ever-changing, inconstant
fashion but with discreet and intelligent variation upon a
single noble theme, contained, and sustained, within the
framework of traditional standards of tested value. There is
always opportunity for personal and individual elegance,
yet it is always dominated by one grand controlling set of
values. This is perhaps the ultimate, and outstanding, im-

pression one receives from Chinese art *in situ* and not fragmented, as we see it in the West, behind the glass cases of museums.

This world of superb design, filled with the light and space of another time and another continent, is not, however, something to be enjoyed merely for its own sake. Far from presenting us with remote and rare pleasures, it is charged with valuable suggestions for use about us, with materials that are ours in the contemporary world. For subtle problems of the handling of volume and geometrical form, for sensitive division of space in both elevation and plan, for simple and graceful refinement of line, it can fairly be said that until the present we have not been wholly ready for some of the best lessons within this mature and wise system. It is we who have needed to develop to the point where examples such as those illustrated in these plates could speak spontaneously for themselves, and at last be understood. What has been evolved from China's long experience fits remarkably well with our needs of today. It can be summed up in a few words: balance, simplicity, and civilization.

NOTES TO THE TEXT

[1] Even a cursory inspection of Chambers' book will show how unobservant, and uninstructed, was the taste of the time. See William Chambers, *Designs of Chinese Buildings, Furniture, Dresses, Machines, and Utensils, Engraved by the best hands from the Originals drawn in China by Mr. Chambers, Architect, etc., London, Published by the Author, etc., 1757.* The author tells us that his work was "done from sketches and measures taken by me at Canton some years ago, chiefly to satisfy my own curiosity."

Thomas Chippendale's much more celebrated work came out in several editions in part earlier and in part later than this. See, however, *The Gentleman and Cabinet-Maker's Director: Being a Large Collection of the Most Elegant and Useful Designs of Household Furniture in the Most Fashionable Taste* by Thomas Chippendale, 3d ed.; London, 1762.

[2] Two series of Chinese illustrations for this novel may be mentioned, both full of suggestions. Here is a mine for the student qualified to work it; and since the pictures speak to the eye direct, they can also be gone over with profit by the reader who does not possess the Chinese language. Their romanized titles are as follows:

(Hsin k'o) *Chin p'ing mei tz'u hua,* in 100 chapters, 21 *ts'ê,* lithograph reproduction of an older edition published in 1933 for the "Ku-i hsiao-shuo k'an-hsing hui" by the Shanghai Chung-yang shu-tien. The format of this edition is small, yet the first *ts'ê* is given over almost entirely to illustrations.

Ch'ing kung chên pao pi mei t'u, in 5 vols., collotype, N.P., N.D. (cir. 1930). These are quite large reproductions of a voluminous series of paintings representing detailed episodes from this novel. Not all are clear, yet at their best they give admirable detail.

The novel itself is of unknown authorship, probably of the sixteenth century.

[3] The interested student here has a special, and extremely complicated, field to investigate. Work was begun in the nineteenth century by Emil Bretschneider, a physician to the Russian legation in Peking, with his *Botanicon Sinicum,* London, Trubner & Co., 1882; and also August Pfiz-

maier (Akademie der Wissenschaften in Wien, Sitzungsberichte, Philos.-Hist. Klasse, vol. 80, 1875, pp. 191–270), *Denkwürdigkeiten von den Bäumen China's*, and vol. 81, 1875, pp. 143–202, *Ergänzungen zu der Abhandlung von den Bäumen China's*.

Since then further knowledge has accumulated in fairly generous measure although it is still not possible to give definitive names for the woods used for the pieces of furniture illustrated in this book. This may well be because there were originally a number of varieties of each group, as must certainly be the case in European cabinetwork, although limited numbers of trade names were apparently used for all; yet many of these trees, or the most prized varieties of them, were, as we have seen, imported, and the record thus escapes us.

Besides these earlier books one may consult the following: Norman Shaw, *Chinese Forest Trees and Timber Supply*, London, T. Fisher Unwin, N.D. (1914); and Ernest Watson, *The Principal Articles of Chinese Commerce (Import and Export)*, The Maritime Customs, II, Special Series: No. 38, 2nd ed., Shanghai, 1930.

Scientifically trained Chinese have also done excellent work in this, a field native to them. See especially Chun Woon Young, *Chinese Economic Trees*, Commercial Press, N.P., N.D. (Shanghai, 1921); Huang Yi-jen, "Chinese Precious Woods," *The North-China Herald*, Shanghai, Nov. 6, 1926, p. 285, and also in *The Chinese Economic Bulletin*, Dec. 18, 1926, p. 358; Tang Yüeh, *Timber Studies of Chinese Trees, Identification of Some Important Hardwoods in Northern China by their Gross Structures*, I, *Bulletin* of the Fan Memorial Institute of Biology, Vol. III, No. 13, Peiping, published by the Institute, July 4, 1932, and also by Tang Yüeh, *Timber Studies of Chinese Trees, Identification of Some Important Hardwoods of South China by their Gross Structures*, I, *ibid.*, Vol. III, No. 17, Nov. 24, 1932; and, finally, Chow Hang-fan, "The Familiar Trees of Hopei," Fan Memorial Institute of Biology, Peiping, *Handbook* No. 4, *The Peking Natural History Bulletin*, 1934.

Dr. J. C. Ferguson's article on "Chinese Furniture" in the *T'ien Hsia Monthly*, March, 1937 (see the working bibliography at the end of this book) should also be mentioned; and Dr. Gustav Ecke in his book of 1944 (see Bibliography) has taken up this matter in detail.

---

[4] This is illustrated by Dr. J. C. Ferguson, Fig. 1a, opp. p. 246, in his *T'ien Hsia Monthly* article of March, 1937, on "Chinese Furniture," given in the working bibliography at the end of this book. The same text was also published as Chap. VIII of his *Survey of Chinese Art*, also in the Bibliography.

⁵ An attempt to trace in any detail how the chair originated in China leads one at once into thorny paths of sinology.

Henri Maspero on page 188 of "La vie privée en Chine à l'époque des Han, *Revue des Arts Asiatiques,* Annales du Musée Guimet, Tome VII, 1931–1932, pp. 185–201, has stated that both the armchair and the folding stool came from the Occident about the third century A.D.; and he does not think that they were much used until the T'ang dynasty.

J. C. Ferguson, in the article titled "Chinese Furniture," in the *T'ien Hsia Monthly* (see Bibliography), places the date a little earlier, saying: "The first chairs were introduced during the reign of Ling Ti, A.D. 168–187, of the Later Han dynasty and were known as *hu ch'uang,* or barbarian couches."

Alide and Wolfram Eberhard in *Die Mode der Han- und Chin-Zeit,* Antwerp, De Sikkel, 1946, p. 88, also think that chairs only appeared about A.D. 150.

The use of the common name of "barbarian couch," familiar even today, in describing large pieces, seems a good reason for thinking that the chair was a true importation, probably from the North. (Wolfram Eberhard has written to the author as of January 16, 1947, that he thinks one reason the Japanese never adopted it is that their culture borrowed comparatively few Northern elements from the Chinese, and that it was from the North that it came in.)

Dr. Gustav Ecke has also dealt with this question, in part, in his article on the folding chair in *Monumenta Serica* (see Bibliography) where he touches on possible Indian origins, pp. 40–47; and also, in part, in his *Chinese Domestic Furniture* (see Bibliography).

For crude chairs, which nevertheless show how the common southern chair could be fashioned from ordinary lengths of bamboo, see Rudolf P. Hommel, *China at Work* (New York: The John Day Co., N.D. [1937], cir. p. 303), published for the Bucks County Historical Society, Doylestown, Pennsylvania.

⁶ Compare on this point the interesting remark of Wilmarth S. Lewis to the effect that "these people" (of the London of 1748) "are about half a foot shorter than the average height of 1941"; *vide* p. 8 of his *Three Tours through London in the Years 1748–1776–1797,* New Haven, Yale University Press, 1941.

⁷ It would have been a charming thing if a book had been put together— when Peking had not yet been occupied, and "modernized," by the Japanese during the last war—of the many rich and unexpected details of Chinese domestic architecture there. Yet this was never attempted.

In the monograph by H. S. Ch'ên and the present author, titled *"Prince Kung's Palace and Its Adjoining Garden in Peking," Monumenta Serica,* Vol. V, 1940, pp. 1–80, with plates and table, an attempt was made to reproduce at least a few photographs of the interiors, completely denuded of furniture though they were, of that palace (perhaps the grandest private residence in the Peking of the later eighteenth and nineteenth centuries); and these plates may be of interest.

Dr. Gustav Ecke somewhat earlier also published an article in German, *"Sechs Schaubilder Pekinger Innenraeume des Achtzehnten Jahrunderts," Bulletin* No. 9, November, 1934, Catholic University, Peking, also mentioned in the Bibliography at the end of the present book, in which he gives plates that are adaptations of an interesting series of European drawings of eighteenth-century Chinese interiors.

Yet this is only the beginning of what should be systematically gathered, from a rich field, if we are to analyze the materials that will yield us the details of this setting.

Mr. Liang Ssu-ch'êng, of the Society for Research in Chinese Architecture, has published one excellent text in Chinese, with plates, on the Ch'ing canon of architecture generally. This is titled *Ch'ing shih ying tsao tsê li, i chung,* text with plates, published by the Chung-kuo ying-tsao hsüeh-shê, Peking, 1934. He has also published, with Liu Chih-p'ing, ten small portfolios of unbound plates giving details for such categories as columns, balustrades, woodwork, etc. The latter are titled *Chien chu shê chi ts'an k'ao t'u chi,* and are also published by the Chung-kuo ying-tsao hsüeh-shê, Peking, 1935, 1936, and 1937. To the student who can command Chinese all these are invaluable; yet even the photographs and cuts alone will be found very useful.

One whole category of Chinese pictures should also be investigated; the *hsing-lê t'u* or depictions of Chinese at their pleasures. Here, often embellished with meticulous detail, we can see in example after example how various settings added to the amenity and interest of Chinese life. This is rich and rewarding material.

Finally, for some idea of the inexhaustible riches of Chinese tracery, the reader should consult Daniel Sheets Dye (Harvard-Yenching Institute Monograph Series, Vols. V and VI), *A Grammar of Chinese Lattice,* 2 vols., Cambridge, Mass.: Harvard University Press, 1937.

2

5

6

7

8

9

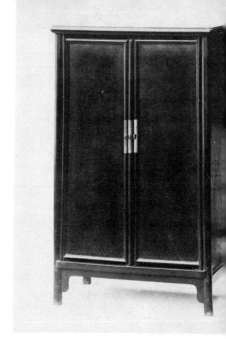

10

11

12

13

14

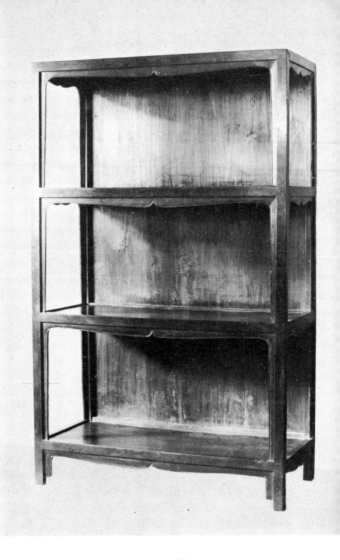

17

18

19

20

21

22

23

24

25

26

27

28

29

30

31

32

33

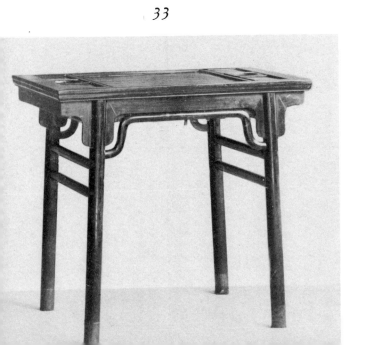

34

35

36

37

38

39

40

41

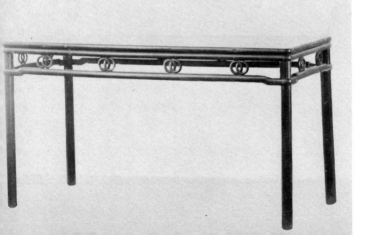

42

43

44

45

46

47

48

49

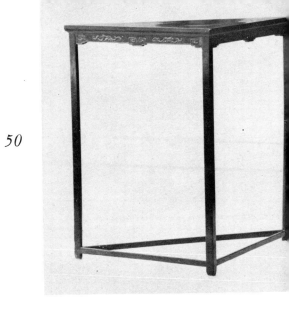

50

51

52

53

54

55

56

57

58

59

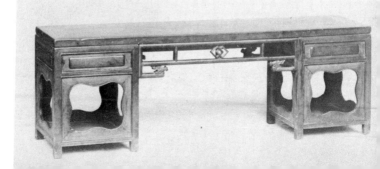

60

61

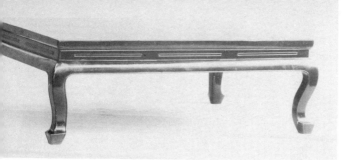

62

63

64

65

66

67

68

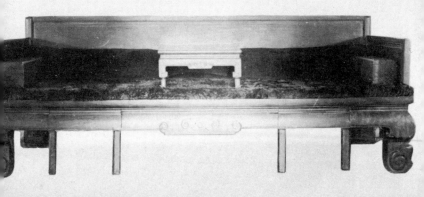

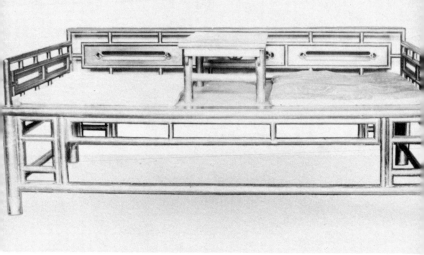

69

70

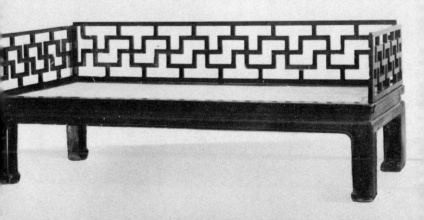

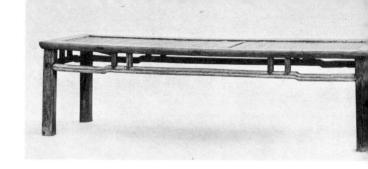

72

73

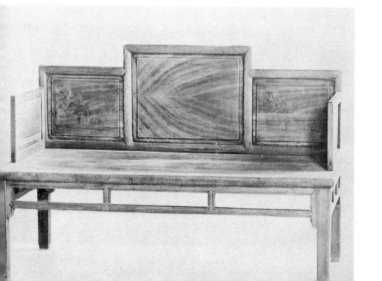

74

75

76

77

78

79

80

81

82

83

84

85

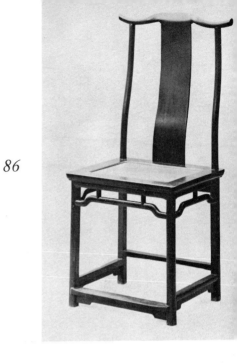

86

87

88

89

90

91

92

93

94

95

96

97

98

99

101

100

102

104

103

105

106

107

108

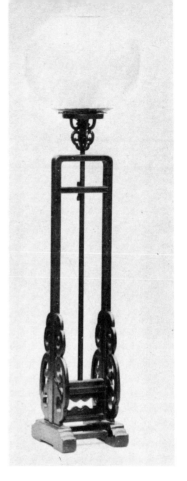

110

109

111

112

NOTES TO THE PLATES

1   SET OF FOUR CUPBOARDS

This is a complete set of four, placed together in the traditional manner, a pair for clothing below and two hat cupboards above. The hinges and lock shields are also of a classic Chinese design, all circular. They are effectively placed, and an effect of polychromy is secured by the use of two woods, one for the framing and another for the flush panels themselves. On all four pieces there is not a single projecting molding.

Wood: *Huang hua-li* with *hua-mu* panels

Full height	8 feet, 6	inches
Breadth (of each)	3 feet, 11	inches
Depth	1 foot, 9⅜	inches

The hat cupboard, above, is 2 feet, 8 inches high.
In the possession of Chinese dealer (Peking).

2   WARDROBE WITH HAT CUPBOARD

These cupboards form one half of a set of four, of a type in which the hinges are not attached to the exterior framing but are set at the edge of a narrow vertical panel, usually secured to the outer frame by pegs within, and removable. Observe the excellent placing of the metalwork on the flat surface, and how it relieves the otherwise complete plainness of the latter by clever variation in its outline. This is an excellent example to illustrate that nicety of adjustment between unduly simple and overintricate design at which the Chinese are masters.

Wood: *Huang hua-li*

Full height	9 feet, 2	inches
Breadth	5 feet, 8¼	inches
Depth	2 feet, 3¾	inches

The hat cupboard, above, is 2 feet, 6 inches high.
In the possession of Messrs. Robert and William Drummond.

3   WARDROBE WITH HAT CUPBOARD

This is another example of half a set of four, narrower, with a combination of rectangular hinges with circular lock shields. It is made of woods less precious than those of the two foregoing examples; yet a horizontal panel of burl, set at the bottom, adds richness to the design. A cupboard such as this often had a removable board flooring slightly below the level of its doors, which covered a convenient blind storage space in which to put seldom-used articles.

> Wood: *Nan-mu* panels, with *ch'iu-mu* sides, the base inset with *hua-mu.*

Full height	7 feet, 5½ inches
Breadth	3 feet, 5¼ inches
Depth	1 foot, 8¾ inches

The hat cupboard, above, is 1 foot, 9½ inches high.
In the possession of Miss C. F. Bieber.

4   WARDROBE WITH TOP CUPBOARD

In these much more sophisticated pieces, the framing members of both the cupboards themselves and of each panel are made slightly concave in cross section while the raised fields of the latter are also given further ornamentation. It can be seen that the wood is of great fineness of texture, waxed to a high luster. The effect is one of great finish, not perhaps of the greatest simple beauty, but completely appropriate for an elegant installation.

> Wood: *Huang hua-li*

Full height	9 feet
Breadth	4 feet, 7½ inches
Depth	2 feet, 3¾ inches

The cupboard, above, is 3 feet high.
In the possession of Dr. Gustav Ecke.

5   WARDROBE WITH HAT CUPBOARD

This is an example, of somewhat less precious woods, in which not only the baseboard is richly carved, although with a discreetly rectangular design but all the panels are also enriched with a narrow frame of ornament. Yet so well is this decoration enclosed within the plain bands of the framework that there is no complication of effect.

Wood: *Ch'iu-mu* with *li-mu* panels

Full height	8 feet, $3\frac{3}{4}$ inches
Breadth	4 feet, 2 inches
Depth	1 foot, 9 inches

The hat cupboard, above, is 2 feet, $8\frac{1}{2}$ inches high.
In the possession of Miss C. F. Bieber.

6 CUPBOARD

This is an example of a design with close affiliation to the Ming tomb models already discussed in the introduction. The bracketed baseboard is of a quite classic type that will be seen in the design of almost every variety of furniture illustrated in this book. The pronounced taper to the piece as a whole is also a commonly used device to accentuate slenderness. A pair of cupboards of this type may, if it is wished, still be set side by side since the top molding does not project beyond the base. The tripartite division of the doorframes, in particular, with top and bottom panels enriched, seems to hark back to a traditional Ming pattern.

Wood: *Nan-mu* inset with *hua-mu*

Height	5 feet, $10\frac{1}{2}$ inches
Breadth at base	3 feet, $\frac{1}{2}$ inch
Breadth at top	2 feet, $11\frac{1}{2}$ inches
(below molding)	
Depth at base	1 foot, 9 inches
Depth at top	
(below molding)	1 foot, $7\frac{1}{2}$ inches

In the possession of Mr. George R. Merrell.

7 CUPBOARD

This is an excellent, simple design with no extraneous element. As in the preceding example, the outer vertical member of each doorframe has projecting dowels that fit into sockets in the framework, and thus serve as hinges. Consequently, except for the metal sheathing about the projections to take the skewer of the conventional padlock, and the ornamental drops that serve as door pulls, no other hardware is needed.

Wood: *Lao yü-mu*

Height	5 feet,	10	inches
Breadth at base	2 feet,	11	inches
Breadth at top	2 feet,	9	inches
(below molding)			
Depth at base	1 foot,	9½	inches
Depth at top			
(below molding)	1 foot,	8	inches

In the possession of Dr. Gustav Ecke.

8   CUPBOARD

This is an even simpler design, also with doors swung on dowels, and flat hardware. Unless it had been very subtly tapered, it would probably have seemed almost mechanical. The note of individuality is in the small hollow oblongs of the hardware drops; otherwise, the eye is left free to enjoy the peerless grain and surface of its fine wood. The effect of the piece is completely functional.

Wood: *Huang hua-li*

Height	5 feet,	7¾	inches
Breadth at base	3 feet,	2	inches
Breadth at top	3 feet,	1	inch
(below molding)			
Depth	1 foot,	7½	inches

Formerly in the possession of the late Dr. E. Schierlitz.

9   CUPBOARD

Very slight elaborations, such as concave profiling of all framing members, including the door panels, and also a small bead rimming the baseboards beneath, are sufficient to give a considerable amount of individuality to this piece. Unlike the three examples of smaller cupboards immediately preceding, this example has neither taper nor central bar, yet it has well-spaced, rectangular metal hinges that go well with its simple vertical framework. It is of a type particularly well suited to contain books or antiques.

Wood: *Huang hua-li*

Height	5 feet, 3 inches
Breadth	2 feet, 8¼ inches
Depth	1 foot, 6½ inches

In the possession of Dr. Gustav Ecke.

10   SMALL CUPBOARD

This is an example lower than those already illustrated, for it is little more than four feet in height, but made according to a familiar general pattern, with both taper and dowel hinges. It, too, is equipped with a removable central bar to make fast the padlock. No less than four materials are used for it: the framework is of light rosewood, the front panels of burl, those at the sides of chicken wing or the so-called satinwood, and the top is of Soochow lacquer. Richness of material here would make any other ornamentation, in the eyes of a good Chinese craftsman, superfluous.

Wood: *Huang hua-li* framework; *hua-mu* front panels; *chi-ch'ih-mu* side panels; Soochow lacquer top

Height	4 feet, 1 inch
Breadth at base	2 feet, 5½ inches
Breadth at top (below molding)	2 feet, 4 inches
Depth at base	1 foot, 5½ inches
Depth at top (below molding)	1 foot, 4¼ inches

In the possession of Dr. Gustav Ecke.

11   SMALL CUPBOARD

Burnished hardware focuses interest upon the center of this piece, here also without the usual central rod. Even though there is somewhat less taper than usual, it is still present. Its pair of openwork metal drops has been designed, obviously, with the plainness of the wood against which they are to be seen kept in mind. There is nearly always, in good pieces like this, a sensitively perceived balance between simple surfaces and a small admixture of delicate ornament to give individuality.

Wood: *Nan yü-mu*

Height	3 feet, 9¾ inches
Breadth at base	2 feet, 4¾ inches
Breadth at top	2 feet, 3¾ inches
(below molding)	
Depth at base	1 foot, 4 inches
Depth at top	1 foot, 3¼ inches
(below molding)	

In the possession of Miss C. F. Bieber.

12 SMALL CABINET

For a small piece made to hold precious objects, this is the ultimate in Chinese design. Its richly carved base, of interesting profile, suggests that it was planned to be placed upon another piece. The panels of burl here contrast very effectively with the framework proper, and it is obvious that the cabinetmaker took their natural richness completely into account. The hardware, never breaking the lines of the design, adds strong necessary accents, effectively drawing it together.

(For measures see Plate 13.)

13 SMALL CABINET (interior)

A photograph of the piece previously illustrated showing the construction of its doors and the arrangement within. The unusual variety and excellent spacing of the drawers should be especially noted. They are made in no less than six sizes, symmetrically placed, and there is also a convenient open shelf at the top. On both exterior and interior the burl and elegant drop handles give unusual richness, yet the design as a whole never departs from sobriety. This would make an ideal collector's cabinet.

Wood: *Chi-ch'ih-mu* with *hua-mu* panels

Height	2 feet, 6¼ inches
Breadth	1 foot, 10 inches
Depth	1 foot, 4¼ inches

In the possession of Miss C. F. Bieber.

14 SET OF FOUR CUPBOARDS

A complete set of four, in another, frequently encountered, and much more elaborate manner, half open but with double-doored cupboards at the bottom of the lower pair and separate upper pieces. The open section is curiously reminiscent of a Provençal *dressoir*. This example is transitional, from the forms already seen to completely open examples. The flanging of the cutout frame on three sides of the open section is decorated in a manner typical of this more ornate style. Similar design is often found—although more frequently in red lacquer picked out with gold than in precious woods—in temple furniture or for other uses where an appeal to tradition was desired.

Wood: *Huang hua-li* with *hua-mu* panels

Full height	6 feet, $5\frac{3}{4}$ inches
Breadth (of each piece)	2 feet, 6 inches
Depth	1 foot, $4\frac{1}{2}$ inches

The small cupboard, above, is 1 foot, $1\frac{1}{2}$ inches high.
In the possession of Mrs. G. von Wolff.

15 OPEN CUPBOARD

This is an excellent example of design for one of a pair of cupboards half open and half closed; and not too costly, for—as the cracking of its panels with age makes clear even in a photograph—it has been made of veneer upon a less precious foundation. The Chinese reserve their esteem for solid, seasoned wood. There is refreshing variety in the shapes used for the open ends of the shelves; and clever relief to the design as a whole is given by the single convenient drawer, as well as by breaking up its solids with the irregular outlines of the metal lock shields. The smaller cupboard has only two doors, but the larger is equipped with the center bar already mentioned. A final detail is a zigzag division of the top shelf, which adjusts the balance of the asymmetrical design. The hinges, as so often, repeat on a smaller scale the same motif as that of the larger pieces of the hardware.

Wood: *Hua-mu* veneer

Height	5 feet, 6¾ inches
Breadth	2 feet, 8½ inches
Depth	1 foot, 1¾ inches

In the possession of Miss C. F. Bieber.

16   BOOK CUPBOARD

Another example, half open and half closed, with an extremely
convenient arrangement of shallow open shelves, two small drawers,
and cupboard below. Modern designers would do well to note that
this simple design is completely freed of rigidity by the clever addition of graceful, slightly curving flanges to the framing of the shelves.
This is probably not a very old piece but certainly a practical one.

Wood. *Hung-mu*

Height	6 feet, 9 inches
Breadth	3 feet, 3¾ inches
Depth	1 foot, 3¾ inches

In the possession of Mrs. Owen Lattimore.

17   BOOKCASE

Here is a practical example of a bookshelf of masterly simplicity.
The central notches in the swing of its gently curved and delicately
bead-molded framing are its only accents of ornament. This framing
goes around three sides of each opening, narrowing in width as it
descends to the level of each shelf and thereby leaving the latter,
at the bottom, unencumbered for use. The same arrangement is
repeated at each end of the piece. Furniture such as this has a quality
of adapting itself comfortably and inconspicuously to any setting in
which it may be placed.

Wood: *Huang hua-li*

Height	5 feet, 3 inches
Breadth	3 feet, 3¾ inches
Depth	1 foot, 5⅜ inches

In the possession of Dr. R. J. C. Hoeppli.

18   PAIR OF SMALL CUPBOARDS

A pair of half-open cupboards, on a smaller scale, balanced and classic in effect. With their convenient combination of three elements—open shelves, small drawers, and cupboards below—such pieces can be most useful in a domestic setting. They allow both for the easy placing of much-used objects, in sight, as well as the stowing away of others. Note how the true rectangular lines of the outline are made to seem tapering by the apparent diminution, achieved by mere outline, of its inner, *hollow spaces*. These also are pieces that, in a mixed grouping, adapt themselves successfully to a great variety of furniture in other styles.

Wood: *Chi-ch'ih-mu*

Height	4 feet, 5 inches
Breadth	2 feet, 1⅛ inches
Depth	11½ inches

In the possession of Miss Mildred Walker.

19   PAIR OF SMALL CUPBOARDS

This is a pair that illustrates perfectly the charm of two asymmetrical pieces juxtaposed. Freedom from excessive regularity is given by the waved flangings to the end openings and by small fretted brackets at the base. The proportion of open to closed surfaces, with a planned lightening of the design at the top, completes the balance. The carved ornament added below is in keepnig with the delicate scale of the whole; these two cabinets are in all only a few inches more than three feet high.

Wood: *Nan-mu*

Height	3 feet, 3 inches
Breadth	1 foot, 10½ inches
Depth	1 foot, ¾ inches

In the possession of Miss C. F. Bieber.

20   SMALL CUPBOARD

A band of "classic" Chinese fretwork, in key pattern, enriches—without overornamenting—the main lines of the design of this small piece. It is another example of the asymmetrical combination of shelf, drawer, and lower cupboard, interesting too because of the contrasting treatment of its sides. Although in a casual piece of this kind the latter were likely to be much in view, they are nevertheless in every detail made a little plainer than the front, or façade, as the photograph clearly shows.

Wood: *Ch'un-mu*

Height	2 feet, 4¾ inches
Breadth	1 foot, 9½ inches
Depth	11⅛ inches

In the possession of Miss C. F. Bieber.

21   SMALL BOOKSHELF

This is an example of an informal open bookstand, with drawers below, of great adaptability to modern use. It is light and spare, yet completely relieved from dullness by the subtle grooving of the moldings of its framework—on the front only, it should be noted, for by contrast the sides are left quite plain. The bead molding on the flanged baseboard and the pair of drops that serve as drawer pulls add desired accents low in the design. Thus a sum of small individual touches, deftly contrived, makes this piece much more than a mere double shelf.

Wood: *Huang hua-li*

Height	1 foot, 11¾ inches
Breadth	1 foot, 1¾ inches
Depth	8¾ inches

In the possession of M. Jean-Pierre Dubosc.

22   CHINESE SIDEBOARD

This is a completely classical example of *lien-san* with all elements complete: curved ends to the top, a feature nearly always present in formal pieces; three shallow drawers beneath (from which it gets its name of three-in-a-row) ; and a generous cupboard at the bottom. In many examples the outer panels of the latter can also be un-fastened by removing wooden pegs from within, for complete ease of access. The bold splay and the robust structure of the piece as a whole are to be noted, as well as the "cloud-head" ornament, of good silhouette, which not only supports the curved ends of the top but helps to lighten the design as a whole. As usual, the placing of the hardware, circular throughout, gives excellent balance. This is a most satisfactory piece of furniture for use in daily living.

Wood: *Chi-ch'ih-mu*

Height	2 feet,	9½ inches
Breadth	7 feet,	2 inches
Depth	1 foot,	8 inches

In the possession of Mrs. E. B. Howard.

23   SMALL ALTAR TABLE

This piece is sometimes called by Peking furniture dealers a *lien-erh,* or two-in-a-row, because of its pair of drawers. It was probably a small altar table, made with ample provision for blind storage space; and has an air of having been specially designed for some elegant family shrine. It is unpretentious but it has just enough formal ornament, principally in its silhouette, and the beaded outline of the cutout panels of its drawers and its front apron, to be suitable for such a use. Perhaps it was used in a private ancestral hall where it could have held incense sticks and similar materials and served, when occasion required it, for dishes of token sacrificial offerings. The cutout on the drawers, a useful device, should be compared with Plate 66.

(For measurements, etc., see Plate 24.)

24   SMALL ALTAR TABLE (rear view)

This is a photograph of the rear of the above, showing a slightly less elaborate apron of different outline. The careful finish of the back lends weight to the supposition that it served a ceremonial purpose, since tables used in an ancestral hall were often freestanding, in front of the altar proper, under a portrait scroll. Here the dead, in the intimacy of a household, could still share the amenities of the living. In spite of this possible use, however, it is a piece that could also be adapted to elegant, if formal, domestic purposes.

Wood: *Huang hua-li*

Height	2 feet, 10½ inches
Breadth	4 feet, 6 inches
Depth	1 foot, 7½ inches

In the possession of Countess Leonore Lichnowsky.

25   SIDEBOARD

A somewhat more rustic, yet very effectively designed, variety of *lien-san,* with blind storage space rather than a cupboard below. Because of its flat top, this is really a very practical piece. Note the bold splay and the rectangular lock shields, with simple bails, wholly in keeping with the general sturdy effect. With only slight adaptation this could make a usable variety of furniture for a modern dining room.

Wood: *Yü-mu*

Height	2 feet, 9 inches
Breadth	5 feet, 1 inch
Depth	1 foot, 6½ inches

In the possession of M. Jean-Pierre Dubosc.

26   CHEST WITH DRAWERS

Here is another variety of *lien-san* design in a very solid and capacious piece. Its effect is different from that of preceding examples because it is rectangular and low, and there is no splay. The excellent quality of its dark wood, even in a veneer finish, also makes its heavy surfaces dignified and formal. The excellent spacing of the hardware on the monochrome plane of the front surface is noteworthy, as is, too, the flanged member supporting the bottom of the framing, which gives the design a necessary lift.

Wood: *Hung-mu* veneer

Height	2 feet, 9 inches
Breadth	6 feet, 1 inch
Depth	1 foot, 8⅝ inches

In the possession of Miss C. F. Bieber.

27 SMALL DRESSER

A solid small dresser, of less precious woods, also in the somewhat more decorated manner that we may provisionally designate as "provincial," although "traditional" might be an equally good name for it. The design and silhouette of the baseboard are—for this style—typical, especially the small hatched and foliated ornament in the center, projecting from the scalloped scroll work. The only moderately successful key pattern on its short legs seems to have been designed in an attempt to relate them in some way with the absolutely plain front. As usual, the placing of the hardware gives quite sufficient ornament to the latter. The burl of the panels makes an effective contrast with the framework; and the small, flat drawers, with their simple, ovoid, brass pulls, are typical.

Wood: *Huai-mu* top; *yü-mu* frame and drawers; *hua-mu* panels.

Height	2 feet, 10½ inches
Breadth	3 feet, 4 inches
Depth	1 foot, 8¼ inches
In the possession of Miss C. F. Bieber.	

28 CHEST WITH DRAWERS

This is a superior chest, designed with a number of carefully calculated subtleties. By keeping the broad, two-doored, lower cupboard absolutely plain and carefully flush with the frame of the whole, and then slightly recessing the plain drawer fronts above—their flat rectangular lock shields set flush—the excellent structural balance of the piece as a whole is even further enhanced. The hardware of the cupboard is sensitively profiled with what the Chinese call "cloudhead" corners, and the carved drops are just sufficiently elaborate to enrich the design. It is remarkable what definite individuality such fine brasswork can confer, when used with plain surfaces of fine hardwood.

Wood: *Huang hua-li*

Height	2 feet, 10 inches
Breadth	4 feet, 2¼ inches
Depth	1 foot, 9¼ inches
In the possession of Dr. Gustave Ecke.	

29   FORMAL SIDE TABLE

Here is a large *t'iao-an,* or formal side table, of a type often used
in the center of the rear wall of the chief apartment in a suite of
rooms. This character is indicated by its upturned ends and by the
carved openwork panels between its supports. Temple and palace
furniture, especially for these larger pieces, was often lacquered, and
its ornamentation also enriched with varieties of metalwork or
mother-of-pearl. For domestic use, however, polished hardwood was
generally considered more fitting. This example, in part of veneer,
shows the technique adopted when a rich effect was devised in a larger
piece—it is over seven feet long—without going to the expense of
using more than a minimum of precious wood.

Wood: *Hung-mu* veneer and *chang-mu*

Height	2 feet, 11	inches
Length	7 feet, 2	inches
Width	1 foot, 8½	inches

In the possession of Mr. George N. Kates.

30   SIDE TABLE

This table is absolutely classical, in the Chinese tradition; and
the model seems to have come down to us, just as it is, through a
number of centuries. One cannot help speculating whether it was
not orignially collapsible, and whether the flanges of its apron did
not serve, in this case, as useful braces. The severely simple dowel
legs are well splayed; and the double cross-struts, also of plain dowel-
ing, form a familiar device in tables of this type to ensure rigidity.
The whole arrangement is seen with such frequency in all varieties
of genre painting that one may call this a basic piece, for use in all
classes of Chinese society.

Wood: *Huang hua-li*

Height	2 feet, 8½	inches
Length	5 feet, 11	inches
Width	1 foot, 9¼	inches

In the possession of Dr. Gustav Ecke.

SIDE TABLE

31

An elaboration of the above, with a slightly heavier table top. The cloud heads, which are a simple device, add a surprisingly rich note of ornamentation; and the legs are elaborated by moldings which accent verticality without altering the silhouette. Thus does Chinese furniture progress in refinement by minor adjustments upon a fundamentally sound basic pattern. When the original design is as uncluttered and structural as this, however, each small change immediately transforms the look of the whole.

Wood: *Hung-mu*

Height	2 feet, 8 inches
Length	5 feet, $3\frac{1}{2}$ inches
Width	2 feet, $2\frac{1}{4}$ inches

In the possession of M. Jean-Pierre Dubosc.

SMALL SIDE TABLE

32

The tables that follow are slighter than the examples already given, yet they show how the basic elements were retained on a diminished scale in the usual Chinese manner. The variations in this collapsible example—for its legs, jointed to fold, give us valuable hints as to the possible structure of the prototype of these trestle tables—are simple and instructive. The silhouette of the ornamented flange under the table top is pulled horizontally outward; the legs are elaborated, with a curious variation, so as to make them seem heavier near the floor; and the lower member of each pair of stretchers is altered in design, and bent down at each end, to add to the effect of structural efficacy. It is by these unexpected changes that a curiously definite character is given to this piece.

Wood: *Huang hua-li*

Height	2 feet, $7\frac{1}{2}$ inches
Length	3 feet, $2\frac{7}{8}$ inches
Width	1 foot, $10\frac{7}{8}$ inches

In the possession of Messrs. Robert and William Drummond.

33   GAME TABLE

This is a small game table, with a removable chess board, etc., and recesses for counters, the whole covered by a plain top not shown in the photograph. To conceal the fact that the sunken recesses of the game equipment project a little beyond the depth of the flanged apron, one further member has been added, and the wood is so fashioned that it assumes almost the quality of bent tubular metal. Otherwise the design is, except for its proportioning, member for member almost identical with that of the example in Plate 30. The pronounced splay markedly lightens the top of the piece, thus preventing it from appearing clumsy; and the effect of the free-standing, bent bracing, repeating the outline of the flanged apron, is most individual.

Wood: *Huang hua-li*

Height	2 feet, 6¾ inches
Length	2 feet, 9½ inches
Width	1 foot, 10½ inches

The board is inlaid with silverwork.

The dimensions of the removable top, not illustrated, are as follows:

Length	2 feet, 10½ inches
Width	1 foot, 11½ inches
Thickness	¾ inches

In the possession of Mr. Robert Winter.

34   SMALL SIDE TABLE

Here is still a further variation; the possibilities are numberless. In spite of its small size, the top of this example has upturned ends; yet a table like this could be used for the display of Chinese scroll paintings, and in that case this device would keep a scroll from falling off when unrolled. The cutout cloud heads of this example, which are completely flat and moldingless, are expanded and given more importance than is usual. The splayed legs and the stretchers, all plain dowels, remain completely in the traditional style; yet a difference in proportioning has transformed the general effect.

Wood: *Huang hua-li*

Height	2 feet,	$9\frac{3}{4}$ inches
Length	3 feet,	2 inches
Width	1 foot,	$6\frac{1}{2}$ inches

Formerly in the possession of the late Dr. E. Schierlitz.

35 SMALL SIDE TABLE

This example, in part of the heavy dark wood known as *tzu-t'an*—a term which literally translated means purple sandalwood, although, as we have seen, blackwood is probably a better equivalent—has particularly instructive variations. The stretchers are here made single rather than double; but the lower parts of the flanged cloud heads, rectangular in silhouette but with rounded corners, add an effect of good support for the table top. Balance has been achieved by another system.

Wood: *Tzu-t'an,* with *hung-mu* panel in top

Height	2 feet,	8 inches
Length	3 feet,	$3\frac{3}{4}$ inches
Width	1 foot,	$1\frac{1}{2}$ inches

In the possession of Mr. George N. Kates.

36 LUTE TABLE

When side tables are small enough to serve as rests for the Chinese zither, or *ch'in,* they are generally called *ch'in cho,* or lute tables, even though they may not actually have been used for this purpose. This is a simple and good example, combining as usual just enough variation from the standard pattern to add refreshment. Note here that a balance has been struck between the rather large squared-off flanges of the apron and the bottom braces, each uniting a pair of the legs; with flanges further transforming the table ends into two vertical, hollow panels.

Wood: *Chi-ch'ih-mu*

Height	2 feet,	9 inches
Length	4 feet,	$1\frac{1}{2}$ inches
Width	1 foot,	$2\frac{5}{8}$ inches

In the possession of Mr. Robert Winter.

37 LUTE TABLE

This is definitely a lute table, arranged with the special elegance to be desired in every appurtenance for an instrument held in such honor by literary men. The oval openings at the sides lighten the design gracefully, and the reticent cloud-head bracketing is just sufficiently complicated to dispel any danger of an oversimple and boardlike effect. Except for bead moldings to pick out the main lines of the piece, there is no other carving. In Chinese eyes this piece of furniture attains a high degree of originality, yet it never violates the canon of restrained variation upon a fundamentally simple, dignified theme. If one can fancy a stringed lacquer lute carefully placed upon the top surface, exactly proportioned so as to hold it, the effect is complete.

Wood: *Huang hua-li*

Height	2 feet, 7½ inches
Length	4 feet, ⅜ inches
Width	1 foot, 3⅝ inches

In the possession of Messrs. Robert and William Drummond.

38 TABLE

Although narrow, this table may well have been designed to be used freestanding, as opposed to the examples already shown, which were more generally placed against walls. It represents the archtype of this variety, reduced to the greatest possible simplicity. Except for its "horse-hoof" legs, a common, popular, Chinese device, it has not a single ornament; it is relieved from absolute rectangularity only by the remarkable delicacy of its proportioning, whereby the inner lines of the tapered legs are discreetly curved in outline at the top so as to join the plain apron without a break.

Wood: *Huang hua-li*

Height	2 feet, 7 inches
Length	4 feet, 8½ inches
Width	1 foot, 6½ inches

In the possession of Dr. Gustav Ecke.

39 TABLE

The oblique braces, placed in plan at an angle of forty-five degrees, as clearly illustrated in this plate, seem an ancient device calculated to bind the legs more firmly, not to the outer framework, but to the central panel of the table top itself. In this example the intentional beveling of these extra ties gives an enhanced effect of rigidity, and they do considerably strengthen actual construction. Otherwise, except for the profiling of the moldings of the table top and the horse-hoof legs already previously mentioned, the design is one of complete simplicity. Observe, however, how springy are the proportions; it is as if inert wood had taken on new life in the cabinetmaker's hands.

Wood: *Huang hua-li*

Height	2 feet, 10¼ inches
Length	3 feet, 7¾ inches
Width	1 foot, 9½ inches

In the possession of **Dr. Gustav Ecke.**

40 TABLE

This is another example without a single extraneous ornament, and only a modified horse hoof, designed to give life to the lower part of the design. Here the top ties furnish the individuality required of the piece. Not a single curving line is used except in the modeling of the feet, yet by careful proportioning an effect of perfect lightness is achieved. As so often, however, it is a detail—here the repeated pairs of short, upright braces between the ties, of broken line, and the table top, all made delicately convex in cross section—that prevents the design from becoming mechanical.

Wood: *Huang hua-li*

Height	2 feet, 8½ inches
Length	4 feet, 4 inches
Width	2 feet, 3 inches

In the possession of **Dr. Gustav Ecke.**

41   TABLE

In the example here illustrated, instead of right angles, all is curves. The top has a double, modified, half-round molding, as if it were reinforced; and the plain dowel legs are also bound together with ties curving in profile, and with a double break, which turn around the corners in a continuing line. This seems to be a motif borrowed from work in native bamboo, where auxiliary members could be cut away on inner surfaces and then bent with steam to make a corner joint fit neatly. The motif of interlaced circles seen in this example is one exceedingly popular with the Chinese, and is found on the greatest variety of objects. It is here skillfully used to bind the ties to the top, allowing for five openings on the long sides and three at the ends. An open space is therefore, in each case, on axis, which effects a further lightening of the design.

Wood: *Hung-mu*

Height	2 feet, 10¼ inches
Length	5 feet, 5 inches
Width	2 feet, 5 inches

Formerly in the possession of the late Hon. Desmond Parsons.

42   TABLE WITH DRAWERS

This is an example of a table with panels filling the slightly recessed spaces between framework and top, another variant. Here the cabinetmaker has concealed two closely fitted drawers, opened from below. A refinement often found in such drawers is a crescent-shaped depression for the finger to catch into, to make the opening sure and easy. The piece displays great delicacy and lightness of form; the shallow drawers have in no way overweighted the design.

Wood: *Huang hua-li*

Height	2 feet, 9¾ inches
Length	4 feet, 2 inches
Depth	1 foot, 10⅝ inches

In the possession of Messrs. Robert and William Drummond.

43   TABLE WITH DRAWERS

Three drawers with metal bails, also in the manner of slightly re-cessed panels, and brackets with just sufficient individuality of profile to avoid bareness, make another variant that is both unpretentious and useful. Here the metalwork also adds the usual note of individ-uality; without it the design would have lacked a needed accent. The horse-hoof feet, too, provide good balance.

Wood: *Huang hua-li*

Height	2 feet, $10\frac{1}{2}$ inches
Length	3 feet, $10\frac{1}{4}$ inches
Width	1 foot, $8\frac{1}{2}$ inches

In the possession of Mrs. Trevor P. Bowen.

44   SMALL TABLE

The range of tables diminishes in scale with every variety of size and proportioning. Here is a smaller example in which the designer has carefully adjusted his proportions to the lighter effect of the whole, the table top still remaining fairly high. The high stretchers, their broken lines adding an effect of resilience, are also wholly typi-cal and effective. Their sharp breaks have even been slightly accented to add the desired special note to the design.

Wood: *Nan-mu*

Height	2 feet, $9\frac{1}{2}$ inches
Length	3 feet, $\frac{3}{8}$ inches
Width	1 foot, $2\frac{1}{2}$ inches

In the possession of Miss C. F. Bieber.

45   SMALL TABLE

Here is another successful solution of the problem of the design of the smaller table. The swinging curves of the apron, notched and once reversed on their way from the center to join the legs without any break whatsoever in line, give spontaneous lightness and ele-gance. The adjustment of the silhouette, at the point of this merging, is adroitly managed. Like examples of the best in modern design, basic simplicity, with a slight amount of carefully calculated elaboration, is enough.

Wood: *Hung-mu* with dark *hua-mu* top.

Height	2 feet, 8 inches
Length	2 feet, 7 inches
Width	1 foot, 2¾ inches

In the possession of Miss Lucile Swan.

46   SQUARE TABLE

Here is what is almost a miniature version of the Eight Immortal table, a traditional name for the square table seating that number of persons. The little blocks of solid carving uniting the ties to the table top are typical of work done during the latter part of the nineteenth century, much of it not in the best of taste. Here they are so placed, on the rise of the stretcher, as to give a useful effect of functional reinforcement. The brackets, instead of supporting the top, like small modillions, are diminished to shallow vertical pins simply to form a helpful transition from leg to superstructure. Another variety of horse-hoof leg is also shown in this table, one that is more nearly square than usual, and with a higher hoof. Here, too, the repertory is capable of great variation.

Wood: *Nan-mu*

Height	2 feet, 4¼ inches
Length	2 feet, 3½ inches
Width	2 feet, 3½ inches

In the possession of Miss C. F. Bieber.

47   SQUARE TABLE

An example of a small square table in which the bracketing is more elaborate, this time making a "stepped" design composed of open, intersected rectangles. These form a good transition to the heavier moldings of the table top, and it should be observed that the lowest member merges in a single plane with the legs themselves. This is an interesting and typical device which draws the design together effectively. As so often elsewhere, the horse-hoof legs add necessary relief, for although the rectilinear bracketing lightens the design, without some curving lines of another variety the effect might have verged on monotony.

Wood: *Huang hua-li*

Height	2 feet, 9½ inches
Length	2 feet, 11 inches
Width	2 feet, 11 inches

In the possession of Messrs. Robert and William Drummond.

48 LOW TABLE

The hardwood of some of the finest smaller tables used in a Chinese interior can be so well burnished that it gives an effect here illustrated. As usual, the design is extremely simple, and the profiling almost millimetric in its careful proportioning. In this example, the legs, in order not to seem to overpower the light, concave surfaces of the rest of the framework—including both stretchers and ties—are divided themselves into two concave channels. The top tie is lightened by the usual device of a double break in its lines upward toward the center. A small bead on the edge of the table top keeps objects from rolling away; and also serves as a finish, almost as if to frame any that might be set upon it. This is a typical refinement.

Wood: *Hung-mu*

Height	2 feet, 3½ inches
Length	2 feet, 8½ inches
Width	1 foot, 7¾ inches

In the possession of Miss C. F. Bieber.

49 LOW TABLE

A more informal design for a very low table, with no moldings whatsoever, even the bracketing being cutout, although with rubbed edges. Its extra shelf is obviously made for convenience; yet even with completely plain legs the design does not seem unduly utilitarian, the brackets adding just enough flavor. One very slight curve is introduced, where the legs merge with the flush, moldingless apron under the top. The cabinetmaker has also allowed himself a little more than the usual play of improvisation in the outline of the brackets, as if to allow their fantasy, in what is otherwise a very simple design, full freedom to make its special effect.

Wood: *Huang hua-li*

Height	1 foot, 10¼ inches
Length	2 feet, 11¾ inches
Width	1 foot, 9½ inches

In the possession of M. Jean-Pierre Dubosc.

50   TRIANGULAR TABLE

Small tables of geometrical shapes are a commonplace in China. Sets of them were made so as to form, when correctly put together, one large square, another version of the old Chinese puzzle. They could then be taken apart to make a great variety of other designs. This triangular example is of a refined, probably quite late, style, with conventional carving on its apron; yet the design as a whole is dignified and has been sensitively carried out. Such a small table could fill a corner unobstrusivey and effectively, its very low stretchers preventing it from appearing unstructural.

Wood: *Hung-mu*

Height	2 feet, 11 inches
Length	3 feet,
Sides	2 feet, 1¾ inches

In the possession of Dr. Gustav Ecke.

51   SEMICIRCULAR TABLE

Semicircular console tables were not used so frequently in China as in Europe, the Chinese seeming to tire far less quickly of large amounts of rectangularity, in a domestic setting, than we do in the West. The example here shown, however, is in every sense classic, and is a good example of how this familiar shape could be handled within the repertory of Chinese design. The legs are merely simple dowels, well placed; and the space division at the top, arranged with small vertical struts bracing the typical ties, is also simple and good. The lowest molding of the table top proper has been made slightly thinner between the legs, a subtle refinement, since it thus repeats the broken line of the ties beneath.

Wood: *Hung-mu*

Height	2 feet, 10 inches
Length	3 feet, 4½ inches
Width at center	1 foot, 8 inches

In the possession of Messrs. Robert and William Drummond.

52 WRITING TABLE

This example comes as near to being the Chinese counterpart of a Western writing desk as any known to the author. It has obvious refinement of proportion, and the absolutely plain drawers, with brass lock shields and copper bails—making for richness of effect through polychromy of metals—are set in a framework also completely unornamented but of extremely sensitive modeling. The tapering outlines of the piece as a whole add lightness. This would also be a useful piece for the additional reason that it is comparatively narrow, although the open space for the knees, under the single drawer in the center, is ample.

Wood: *Huang hua-li*, with *hung-mu*

Height	2 feet, 9¾ inches
Length	5 feet, ¾ inch
Depth	1 foot, 10¾ inches

In the possession of Mr. George N. Kates.

53 WRITING TABLE

Here is another long and narrow example with a central drawer, only here set between two single deeper ones instead of between pairs superimposed as in the preceding example. Lest this arrangement appear oversimple, a certain amount of pierced bracketing has been used, in a traditional design coming down the ages, scarcely changed from patterns such as may be found on ancient bronzes. These few small pieces of wood give to this writing table much character; and the little keyhole shields on its drawers, shaped like small vases, add a late, yet pleasant, final touch.

Wood: *Huang hua-li*

Height	2 feet, 6¾ inches
Length	4 feet, 8½ inches
Depth	1 foot, 10⅞ inches

In the possession of M. Jean-Pierre Dubosc.

54   COLLAPSIBLE DESK

There is one type of writing table that seems to have been used completely and solely as such: the official's collapsible desk for traveling. The mandarin on circuit, living in bare rooms and often away on long journeys, often took with him a certain number of objects to retain some of his quality of a learned man, if merely by their flavor, even in the wilderness. In Peking one formerly could rummage for traveling lamps, traveling libraries in wooden cases, and miscellaneous furnishings for traveling. This example is typical. The central section of the top, demountable, is made of two transverse narrow pieces; and the boxlike upper ones at the ends can be stowed, with these, into the lower compartments, like children's building blocks. Thus when packed, the whole becomes merely two filled containers which could be transported on a single carrying pole. The design has nevertheless made possible a good piece of furniture, sensible and useful when set up, as shown in the accompanying plate.

Wood: *Nan-mu*

Height	2 feet,	8¾ inches
Length	4 feet,	2¼ inches
Depth	2 feet,	2½ inches

In the possession of Mr. Theodore D. Starr, Jr.

55   COLLAPSIBLE DESK

Here is another variant of the same type of traveling desk, also with shallow, transverse pieces forming the central portion. These are attached, with projecting flat pins fitting into slots, to the half-open, half-solid members forming the ends. As usual, the whole construction, when collapsed, goes into the two bottom compartments. The doors to the latter also have small pins below, which fit into the bottom of the frame; they are thus not hinged but simply removable. The two central drawers go the full depth of the piece and must be pulled out before it is collapsed.

Wood: *Chi-ch'ih-mu*

Height	2 feet, 11	inches
Length	4 feet, 4	inches

Depth: upper section	2 feet, 1¾ inches
Depth: lower section	2 feet, 5 inches
Height: lower section	1 foot, 10½ inches

In the possession of Miss Beatrice M. Kates.

56   DESK

Here is an example of a writing table that is sectional rather than collapsible. It is made up of two commodes with a central table, equipped with similar drawers, fitted in between; and although the lower struts in the center are not especially to be recommended unless one desires a footrest, this piece offers many ideas for the modern designer of module furniture. The repeating drawers, with identical hardware—here a Chinese version of the familiar European lock shield, in the form of a bat, with a covered keyhole—tie the design into a single composition, integrating it perfectly. The small cupboards beneath are also convenient; they are hinged on wooden pins like the larger wardrobe doors already seen.

Wood: *Nan-mu*

Height	2 feet, 11¼ inches
Length	4 feet, 7¼ inches
Depth	2 feet, 3¾ inches
Width of central section	2 feet, 3¾ inches
Width of side section	1 foot, 1¾ inches

In the possession of Miss C. F. Bieber.

57   DESK

This desk has the same number of drawers front and back, going only half way through it in depth, so that it can be used freestanding by two people. It, too, is demountable rather than collapsible, and is transitional to a type to be illustrated in several of the following plates. The top is of one long single piece, merely resting upon the two commodelike bases. The paneling and hardware, repeated on all three pieces, give the design homogenity; and although the force of gravity alone keeps the top in place, the piece gives no impression of impermanence. The flangings on the lower part of each pedestal, now quite familiar, serve to keep small objects in place and are thus useful as well as helpful to the general design.

Wood: *Yü-mu*

Full height	2 feet, 9¾ inches
Length	4 feet, 8 inches
Depth	2 feet, 10½ inches
Side sections: height	2 feet, 1¼ inches
Side sections: width	1 foot, ¼ inch
Side sections: depth	2 feet, 10½ inches

In the possession of Miss C. F. Bieber.

58   SMALL TABLE (with board and supports)

An example of demountable, "box and board" furniture like the preceding plate in that it is composed of a top merely resting upon two supports, yet unlike it in that this top is merely a single plank. This variety of side table possibly has a very old history; the range goes from giant lacquered palace pieces, so long that at times the thick top "board" is a built-up facsimile, hollow and lighter, to small and slender examples like the one here illustrated. In general, the Chinese valued highly a single piece of superior wood for this popular type, and for this reason it is today often possible to find the supports remaining when this central member has been removed for other purposes. Observe the ease with which ornamentation has been secured—merely flat cutout aprons under each drawer and shelf. The panels for the drawers are further given a slight projection in the thickness of the wood. These are the usual details varied a little in order to avoid monotony.

Wood: *Huang hua-li*

Full height	2 feet, 1 inch
Full length	5 feet, 4½ inches
Full width	11¾ inches
Side Sections:	
Height	1 foot, 11⅝ inches
Breadth	11¾ inches
Depth	11¾ inches

In the possession of Dr. Gustav Ecke.

59   LOW DEMOUNTABLE TABLE

Here is a demountable piece that also uses the "box and board"
principle, one for use upon the *k'ang* itself. Besides the top, of a single
board, and the pair of supports, it also has a further demountable
framework, pegged into the latter, which helps to unify the composition as a whole. Here again we have what is a smaller version of a
design used in many other scales. In humbler houses, where bedding
was folded away during the day and placed at the back of the family
k'ang, it might well have been placed on a similar, probably somewhat less precious, piece. Yet the guest *k'angs* in reception rooms
were often equipped with quite elaborate furniture for varied bric-
a-brac, which might also have been displayed on such an example as
this, because the Chinese considered it elegant to place a single piece
of porcelain or bronze in a framed, hollow recess like that at the base
of each support.

Wood: *Chi-ch'ih-mu*

Height	1 foot, 5½ inches
Length	4 feet, 6 inches
Width	1 foot, 1½ inches

In the possession of Mrs. M. R. Sickman.

60   LOW TABLE

The low table, as we have seen, is one variety of Chinese furniture
that can be traced to remote antiquity. In its earliest form it seems
to have been made up of four solid surfaces, rather than with legs,
so that it resembled a small platform; but even at an early date,
when the arrangement of a top merely supported by two upright
ends is found, the joining edges were apparently often slightly
rounded, as in this example. The stretchers at the bottom of each
end carry out the archaic effect, completing the framing. The design
is thus similar to the earlier prototype, only hollow.

Wood: *Hung-mu* with lacquer top

Height	1 foot, 1½ inches
Length	2 feet, 11¾ inches
Width	1 foot, 2¼ inches

In the possession of Dr. Otto Burchard.

61   *K'ANG* TABLE

A simple, excellently designed example of *k'ang* table with the traditional horse-hoof legs, which come in the greatest variety of curved outline. They run the gamut from the almost straight, to examples elastically profiled as here, or swung gracefully out and back again. One practical advantage of this traditional form, which turns in, was that it had no projections that might catch the garments of users seated cross-legged in the old-fashioned manner. The profiling of the outline is made more effective by swellings convex in cross section, and also by a fine bead molding which makes a line of light on the polished wood. This is quite enough to give such a piece due character. A convenient little drawer has been inset at the side, completely flush with the molded surfaces.

Wood: *Huang hua-li*

Height	11½ inches
Length	2 feet, 10¼ inches
Width	1 foot, 11¾ inches

In the possession of Dr. Gustav Ecke.

62   *K'ANG* TABLE

The cabriole leg, as here illustrated, is on the whole not very common as a motif in Chinese furniture; yet it does exist, and can be treated with much sensitiveness both in form and line. It is definitely less typical, however, than the horse-hoof variety of the preceding plate. The elongated vents, or slits, in the collar under the table top, are a device frequently used to lighten or enrich an otherwise dull surface, and are part of the classical repertory.

Wood: *Hung-mu*

Height	1 foot, 1¾ inches
Length	3 feet, 4¾ inches
Width	2 feet, 3 inches

In the possession of M. Jean-Pierre Dubosc.

63 *K'ANG* TABLE

An example that is only seemingly plain, for it has concealed drawers set in its sides. These are made with vents in a double, outer drawer front to serve as pulls. The arrangement offers a practical motif for Western design, as yet little used. The satisfying splay of the plain, sturdy dowel legs gives the otherwise low design a helpful amount of spring. The rounded *ni chiao,* or "eel corners" of the table top, as the Chinese call them, furnish another example of how effectively every detail is adjusted, in furniture as carefully designed as this, to contribute to the effect of the whole. Sharpness of line is here gracefully avoided.

Wood: *Huang hua-li*

Height	1 foot
Length	2 feet, 9 inches
Width	1 foot, 6¾ inches

In the possession of Miss Mabel E. Tom.

64 *K'ANG* TABLE

Here is an attractive example, perhaps for slightly humbler use than the *k'ang* tables already shown. In the traditional setting of a household of quality, the general arrangement was to place a well-polished table in the middle of the *k'ang* so that two seated people, usually host and guest, could share it between them, one on each of the long sides. This example with its simple drawers belongs definitely to a less formal variety, and might well have been used against a wall to hold small household necessities. With convenient pieces like this for needed objects, the *k'ang* could be used in uncluttered comfort.

Wood: *Huang hua-li* with *hua-mu* top

Height	11 inches
Length	2 feet, 3½ inches
Width	1 foot, 3¾ inches

In the possession of Mrs. G. von Wolff.

65   *K'ANG* TABLE

We terminate this series with an example which to European eyes distinctly evokes the name of Chippendale. It is nevertheless completely free of those aberrations which became associated with that style. The fretwork between tie and top is spare, yet satisfying, lightened in its central open panel simply by the omission of all ornament. If studied with this canon of taste in mind, Chippendale might well be re-evaluated with profit. Rectilinear space division, as here practised by the Chinese, has surely never elsewhere been surpassed. This piece presents fruitful suggestion for the contemporary designer in search of motifs for low tables; and Western borrowings, it may be said, have as yet not begun to exhaust the possibilities of the Chinese repertory of geometrical tracery.

Wood: *Huang hua-li*

Height	$11\frac{1}{4}$ inches
Length	2 feet, $11\frac{1}{2}$ inches
Width	1 foot, 9 inches

In the possession of Miss Mildred Walker.

66   *K'ANG* CUPBOARD

The *k'ang* was used so much in daily living that larger pieces were also essential to its furnishing. Here is an example, equipped with a central cupboard, and also a pair of drawers, designed so that there is additional space for blind storage below. Folded quilts were ordinarily piled upon the top during the day. The ornamentation of the drawers, a simple cutout, enriched only with a simple bead, is applied to the front surface in such a way that when the drawer is closed it comes flush with the otherwise completely plain front of the piece as a whole. This is a Chinese device long in familiar use, as may be seen in Plate 23. Well-placed hardware provides the only additional element desired for a piece of this kind. The Chinese display great affection for unornamented surfaces, allowing the contrasting grains of plain framework and flush panels to display their own natural richness.

Wood: *Nan-mu*

Height	1 foot, 6½ inches
Breadth	4 feet, 6 inches
Depth	1 foot, 5 inches

In the possession of Mr. George N. Kates.

67   *K'ANG* CUPBOARD

Here is a much more elaborate example of *k'ang* cupboard designed for more formal use, with five small drawers above and a single cupboard, with doubled square doors and recessed paneling, extending almost the full length of the piece below. Although there is also a band of rich carving at the base, the tripartite horizontal design is controlled throughout by sober structure and capable framing. In the selection made for this book there are few examples as ornamented as this, yet it proves that in good hands even comparatively late design, which this is, was quite strong enough to dominate the elaboration of subsidiary members. The brasswork, as usual, is sensitively planned to enhance the general effect.

Wood: *Nan-mu* top; *li-mu* with *lao hung-mu* drawers

Height	1 foot, 5 inches
Breadth	3 feet, 9 inches
Depth	1 foot, 5½ inches

In the possession of Mrs. G. von Wolff.

68   CANOPIED BED

The type of large canopied Chinese bed here shown is familiarly illustrated in numberless paintings, usually equipped for use with a shallow mattress, folded quilts, and hard pillows; its curtains were often held up during the day by large sickle-shaped hooks, generally of metal, enriched with pendant tassels. This is a good example, with all the members of its cabinetwork complete. A shallow footstool running the whole length of the piece was often further provided. The light railing above the platform, running around all but the center of the front, gave the cabinetmaker a chance to show the range of his skill; and one can find the greatest variety of patterns in delicate, but not flimsy, joinery. Virtuosity was here given fullest play, as this example shows. Notice how adequately the canopy is supported by simple vertical uprights, braced with light stretchers.

Wood: *Huang hua-li*

Height	7 feet, 10 inches
Length	7 feet, 5¼ inches
Width	5 feet, 1½ inches

In the possession of Dr. Gustav Ecke.

69   LARGE WOODEN *K'ANG*

Although the built-in brick bed, or *k'ang,* is normal to North China, it is not used exclusively. Wooden *k'angs,* which we should perhaps call couches or day beds—almost universal in the South, although generally made of much thinner material—are also often found. When of the extremely solid, heavy type shown in the accompanying plate, they become quite naturally one of the chief pieces of furniture in a reception room, and naturally dominate it in their dignity and size. Here the heavy legs, with their curious, reversed profiling, and the absolutely plain back- and side-boards, emphasize the scale of the piece.

This example, said to be for luxurious opium smoking, may indeed have been so used since its supplementary pairs of small legs, supporting sliding extensions, made it possible for two persons to recline at full length. The matching small *k'ang* table is here shown at proper height and in proper position, as are, too, the square elbow cushions of woven rattan, which are a part of its formal furnishing.

Wood: *Pai-mu*

Height	3 feet, 6¾ inches
Height to arms	3 feet
Length	9 feet, 11 inches
Width	4 feet, 2 inches
Small table in center	
Height	11 inches
Length	3 feet, ½ inch
Width	2 feet, ½ inch

In the possession of Mr. Robert Winter.

70   WOODEN *K'ANG*

Here is a contrasting, much slenderer piece of the same type, closely related to Southern work in bamboo which it simulates in more precious wood, especially in its imitation of what would have been canes of slighter stock in the subsidiary members of its framing. Many members are made round in cross-section, and corners are also rounded. Among its best details are the cutout groovings in the suspended rear panels. The effect of the whole is summery and light so that it is a perfect piece for warm weather or for a garden pavilion. With its matching small *k'ang* table, an integral part of the design, this is indeed a pleasant piece of furniture made to be used for sociability by two people. Westerners almost invariably add cushions or other upholstery as here shown, yet the seat is provided with a fine variety of close-woven cane matting stretched tight over solid boards. In general, the Chinese use a piece like this with little else.

Wood: *Chi-ch'ih-mu*

Height of back	2 feet,	7¾ inches
Height of arms	2 feet,	5½ inches
Height of seat	1 foot,	8½ inches
Length	6 feet,	8½ inches
Width	3 feet,	10½ inches

In the possession of Messrs. Robert and William Drummond.

71   WOODEN *K'ANG*

Here is an example displaying a geometrical purity highly prized in Chinese eyes. It is to be observed that the base is massive and simple, with staunch horse-hoof legs outlined with a strong bead and no further elaboration. The woven seat is slightly recessed and completely plain. It is at the back and sides that the cabinetmaker has displayed his skill with solid and substantial joinery, yet he has employed a single pattern only, the swastika—with Buddhist allusions—so universally used in China. The two ends of the piece are a trifle lower than the back, yet they repeat the same design on a slightly diminished scale. It is to adjustments as delicate as these that the developed style can lead, where even fractions of an inch alter the final effect. Sober geometry here reaches definitive form; beyond this ultimate point refinement cannot go.

Wood: *Huang hua-li*

Height	2 feet,	7 inches
Length	6 feet,	8¼ inches
Width	3 feet,	⅞ inches

In the possession of Dr. Gustav Ecke.

72   COUCH

Here is a much less formal *chu'un t'a,* or "vernal couch," a light piece to be moved into the open air and sun when the season for its use arrives. Such benches, in coarse materials, are very common to the South for warm weather, but they are also found in North China for use during the summer. The top is here made of thin, slightly convex, polished bamboo slats, like xylophone keys, laid between two grooves in the sides of the framework. Their glossy, natural finish, which is damp repellent, is most agreeable to the touch. The arrangement is also self-ventilating, a good example of Chinese ingenuity in making the most of natural qualities of materials. This example is somewhat finer in design and execution than an ordinary bench for this practical use, and is satisfyingly proportioned. The small vertical struts bracing the long ties come in pairs, forming hollow squares, which become in their turn a further ornament. The ties are also outlined so as to seem double, thus reinforcing the effect of the design.

Wood: *Hua-li* with bamboo slats

Height	1 foot,	7 inches
Length	6 feet,	½ inch
Width	1 foot,	9¾ inches

In the possession of Miss C. F. Bieber.

73   SMALL COUCH

An interesting intermediate example, half way between couch and chair, its paneling of rhythmically descending heights kept severely plain. Ties with plain uprights only are used beneath its seat of solid wood. This piece seems a little too wide for an ordinary single seat, although it may be said that those of the Emperor, in Ch'ing times, even if rustic—as might have been the fancy for one of the many studies or pavilions for the enjoyment of "nature" in palace gardens such as those toward the Western Hills, near Peking, or for the summer in Jehol—were of course ample; and any dignitary could have something wider than the ordinary chair. Chairs of state were naturally wide, even if they had to be filled in by large, often elaborate cushions. Perhaps the example in this plate, however, was merely a small seat built to measure for some exiguous space and for household use.

Wood: *Pai-mu*

Height of back	2 feet, 10¼ inches
Height of arms	2 feet, 3¼ inches
Height of seat	1 foot, 5 inches
Length	4 feet, 5¾ inches
Width	2 feet, 1¾ inches

In the possession of Mr. Robert Winter.

74 ARMCHAIR

This is the so-called "lohan" type of Chinese chair; and since the lohan were the saints and sages of Buddhism, which was introduced to China from India, it may be indeed that the name harks back to an Indian origin. It is a completely typical example built high, with a stretcher at the front designed to keep feet from the floor in a cold climate, and with a generous, rounded back rail. Its arms project slightly beyond the vertical prolongations of the front legs, all of which become supports above the level of the seat. The knobbed ends to such curved rails can be seen peeping out from under the throw-overs of furs or brocade in any number of Chinese ancestor paintings. Very typical is the curving apron under the front of the seat, which is extended to form a flange going down the side of each leg. This is quite broad at the front of the chair but is also repeated on a slightly smaller scale at the sides. With the marked splay of its front legs, and the addition of this reinforcing member, such a chair may be said to display all the characteristic elements of the type. The base is much more sturdy than that of similar chairs in the West, suggesting that it may first have existed as a variety of stool, to which the supports at back and sides were later added.

Wood: *Huang hua-li*

Full height	3 feet, 3¼ inches
Breadth	1 foot, 11¼ inches
Depth	1 foot, 6½ inches
Height to arm	2 feet, 4½ inches
Height to seat	1 foot, 8 inches

In the possession of Dr. Gustav Ecke.

75   ARMCHAIR

Another lohan chair, with a typical curved back rail ending in the usual knoblike projections. The plain, unornamented splat at the rear is here of double curvature, unlike that in the preceding example; and although the back rail is supported by uprights at the rear corners, also contrived as prolongations of the back legs, the curved pair of supports at the front are set back, and there are no intermediate ones. The shallow aprons, on all four sides, bracing and strengthening the seat and legs, are of a type used again and again for this purpose. Unornamented legs, well slanted, and plain stretchers complete the sensible design, which for all its sobriety is never rigid.

Wood: *Huang hua-li*

Full height	3 feet, ¾ inch
Breadth	1 foot, 10½ inches
Depth	1 foot, 6 inches
Height to seat	1 foot, 6¾ inches

In the possession of Miss C. F. Bieber.

76   ARMCHAIR

Here is a very solid example of the same type. The curved back rail, here rectangular in section and giving an effect of much strength, descends to the chair seat in an unbroken curve so as to form both back and arms in one. It is nevertheless quite adequately supported by the splat and by a single pair of uprights at the rear corners. The low-relief lotus ornament on this splat is in traditional style, ingeniously carved so as to seem half inset. Note how flexible and pliable the wood of the rail is made to appear, its flowing lines and multiple curvature presenting no apparent problem to the craftsman. The seat is of polished wood instead of cane on a wood base; and the front stretcher serves, as usual, for a footrest. As in other examples, it shows that it has been worn with time. Careful housewives used to cover this crosspiece with a section of curved bamboo, which was snapped or tied into place, in order to prevent undue scuffing, but it could be removed before the arrival of honored guests.

Wood: *Li-tzu-mu*

Full height	3 feet, 1 inch
Breadth	1 foot, 11 inches
Depth	1 foot, 5¼ inches
Height to arm	2 feet, 2 inches
Height to seat	1 foot, 7½ inches

In the possession of Miss C. F. Bieber.

77   ARMCHAIR

Here is the same lohan type, but in a slenderer, rather highly decorated variant. The sloping curve of the back rail has not undergone any change, yet both it and all its supporting members have been made considerably finer and slighter in proportion. The legs, too, are light, although the usual splay lends them strength. The splat, of double curvature, has the usual single carved ornament and also two typical flanges,—an ancient device. Beneath the front and side stretchers, an additional member has been added, bent so as seemingly to support them. Finally, the front brackets below the seat--although not the side or rear ones—have been carved with openwork cloud heads. Thus a number of comparatively small variations transforms the character of the piece, refining it until a totally different effect is given from those of the preceding examples.

Wood: *Huang hua-li*

Full height	3 feet, 4 inches
Breadth	2 feet, ¾ inch
Depth	1 foot, 7 inches
Height to seat	1 foot, 8½ inches

In the possession of Countess Leonore Lichnowsky.

78   ARMCHAIR

Another variety of chair, here illustrated, is called the *kuan mao,*
or "official's cap" chair, since the two projecting ends of its flat top
rail were fancied to resemble the narrow, wired or starched bands
that projected from formal headdresses of Chinese civil officials in
pre-Ch'ing times. The details of the lower part of this type are often
identical with examples already shown, as is also the arrangement of
the arms and the plain splat. The chief difference is that the official's
cap chair has a square rather than a rounded back. The example here
illustrated has a lower superstructure than is general; yet in many
old paintings a similar, movable back rest for use on a low platform
is represented so much like this that one is tempted to ask whether
varieties of the chair in China may have developed merely through
the addition of it—first low and gradually higher—to the ordinary
stool. This would explain what might otherwise seem the excessively
heavy base of most chairs in the traditional style.

Wood: *Huang hua-li*

Full height	2 feet, 10 inches
Breadth	2 feet
Depth	1 foot, 6 inches
Height to arm	2 feet, $3\frac{1}{2}$ inches
Height to seat	1 foot, $7\frac{1}{2}$ inches

In the possession of Miss C. F. Bieber.

79   ARMCHAIR

This example represents a more normal proportioning of the official's cap type of armchair. All its vertical lines bend inward as they
rise, lightening the design; and the splay of the front legs is greater
than that of the back, a feature present in most of the chairs already
illustrated. The double curvature of the splat and the small flangelike bracing members inserted under the arms are also to be observed.
The projecting top rail, it should be said, helped to accommodate
an ample width of fabric, which in earlier days was commonly
thrown over both back and seat and allowed to descend toward the
floor. In such cases, a footstool was often further provided, perhaps
itself brocade covered. When thus equipped, the chair became a seat
of honor, and was conceived merely as a foundation for this further

arrangement, fitting it for the use of some dignitary. In the present example it should be observed that the front stretcher, although of hardwood, has been worn by long use.

Wood: *Huang hua-li*

Full height	3 feet,	9	inches
Breadth	1 foot,	8¾	inches
Depth	1 foot,	7	inches
Height to seat	1 foot,	8	inches

In the possession of Miss C. F. Bieber.

80 ARMCHAIR

Certain Chinese chairs, as anyone who has traveled the Chinese countryside knows, are strikingly massive in proportion, and obviously have been made very durable to stand hard wear. The example here illustrated is fairly representative of this type, where each member is of great solidity. Such a piece can actually be exceedingly heavy. When equipped with perhaps not only a throw-over but also with seat cushions, it might also serve for traveling officials—perhaps come from a distance to pronounce on local grievances—who could be installed for hearings in dignity and comfort. Such sessions of countryside justice often took place under porches open to a courtyard to accommodate the official's train, his guards and runners, and the townsfolk. It was also customary to place a large screen, often of a single broad panel upright in a wooden frame, behind the seat of honor, as countless old pictures show. Indeed, living with many open walls to their buildings, the Chinese historically seem to have used these screens as part of normal furnishing. Except behind thrones in palaces, practically none now survive, and many were probably frail; yet miniature models, and occasionally examples made up of panels inset with stone or precious woods, nevertheless transmit the type.

Wood: *Huang hua-li*

Full height	3 feet,	5¼	inches
Breadth	2 feet,	1½	inches
Depth	1 foot,	7⅜	inches
Height to arm	2 feet,	5	inches
Height to seat	1 foot,	7¾	inches

In the possession of Messrs. Robert and William Drummond.

81   SMALL ARMCHAIR

In any Chinese apartment to be occupied by a person of rank, it was customary to place the chair for that person absolutely in the center against the rear wall, which was often windowless. It thus became a little chair-of-state. This example is quite typical of what might be used for such a purpose, even though its lack of width would preclude its employment for a personage of high rank in a formal setting. It must be remembered that the typical Chinese palace had a great many apartments, and in each of those destined for the use of the owner, there was necessarily a throne, or "precious seat," as the Chinese call it. In this example three juxtaposed hollow panels, placed together vertically, form the stepped back, while one of the same design, turned at right angles, makes the arms. The piece is rather small, perhaps used by a woman; and its front stretcher, which also serves as footrest, almost touches the ground.

Wood: *Chi-ch'ih-mu*

Full height	3 feet, 2 inches
Breadth	1 foot, 11½ inches
Depth	1 foot, 7¼ inches
Height to arm	2 feet, 3¼ inches
Height to seat	1 foot, 7½ inches

In the possession of Mrs. M. R. Sickman.

82   ARMCHAIR

Many square-backed chairs do not have official's cap projections; the uprights of the back are smoothly merged in one continuous line with the top rail, leaving a slight depression in the center, at the top of the splat, to accommodate the nape of the neck. This is managed with such ease that the effect is almost as if the wood had grown in this way. Here is an excellent example in which the whole plane of the upper part of the back is bent slightly backward, and the arms, too, are gently curved to accommodate the human figure. When a number of such refinements are united, as in this example, the result is a civilized piece of furniture. The general effect is only emphasized by the use of highly polished hardwood, with just enough irregularity of grain showing through the finish to add interest.

Wood: *Huang hua-li*

Full height	3 feet, 7 inches
Breadth	1 foot, 11¼ inches
Depth	1 foot, 5⅜ inches
Height to arm	2 feet, 5 inches
Height to seat	1 foot, 7½ inches

In the possession of Dr. Gustav Ecke.

83 CHAIR

Chairs without arms exist in great numbers in China; and in assigning seats according to rank, they naturally formed the variety intermediate between armchair and simple stool. The type shown here, with a tripartite division of its splat such as is often seen in Ming and Ch'ing painting and woodcut, is in style also related to the Ming tomb models mentioned in the Introduction. The apron, on the front face only, with its elaborate stalactitelike outline, shows how very much emphasis the Chinese think it fitting to give to frontality. The sides are relatively much plainer; yet this seems more natural when it is remembered that according to formal arrangement, in which they were always to be placed, Chinese chairs were not made to be looked at consciously except from the front. Even tables, as we have seen, often had an apron of fabric fixed to them, covering the face opposite the spectator.

Wood: *Nan-mu*

Full height	3 feet
Breadth	1 foot, 10 inches
Depth	1 foot, 5½ inches
Height to seat	1 foot, 8 inches

In the possession of Miss C. F. Bieber.

84 CHAIR

Here is the official's cap back rest in a model designed without arms. The breadth of the seat and the ever-present slight tilt of the legs give the design its stability. The gradual outward curve of the back, bending the head rail until it is slightly off vertical at the top, relieves the design from stiffness, and for Westerners makes for somewhat greater comfort. In general, the Chinese seem quite content with chairs of this type that are completely upright and rigid, and wholly lacking in upholstery. The subsidiary small apron at the very bottom under the front stretcher, it should be observed, pulls the design of the base down toward the front.

Wood: *Chi-ch'ih-mu*

Full height	2 feet, 10 inches
Breadth	1 foot, 8½ inches
Depth	1 foot, 4⅞ inches
Height to seat	1 foot, 5¾ inches

In the possession of Miss C. F. Bieber.

85 CHAIR

Here is a model not very different from the above, which is provided with what might be termed a "hollow splat," making for firmness and lightness combined. The slightly back-tilted top rail is terminated by a member circular in cross section, which helps to give relief from what might otherwise be too rectangular a design. This makes feasible the complete simplicity of the stretchers and struts directly under the seat, although the lowest front stretcher also has a secondary supporting member beneath, with an outline that is intentionally broken. This is a compact, light piece of furniture, and one that can be handled easily.

Wood: *Hung-mu*

Full height	2 feet, 10½ inches
Breadth	1 foot, 8½ inches
Depth	1 foot, 4½ inches
Height to seat	1 foot, 6½ inches

In the possession of Mr. Harold Acton.

86 CHAIR

This yoke-back chair has ties below its seat that by their sharply curving outlines—harmonizing with the top rail—give a specially resilient effect to the design as a whole. When chairs and tables are made to match, it is such a motif that is usually the one repeated, tying a set together and giving it uniformity of character. In this example, the top rail has been quite deeply scooped out to fit the nape of the neck, and the back actually bends in slightly at the top. This is a not uncommon device, intended, however, for a person of small stature.

Wood: *Huang hua-li*

Full height	3 feet, 7½ inches
Breadth	1 foot, 7¼ inches
Depth	1 foot, 3¾ inches
Height to seat	1 foot, 8½ inches

In the possession of Dr. Gustav Ecke.

87 ## CHAIR

A last example, without arms, relying upon the contrasting curves of its framing, upon the flanges of the aprons on all four sides under its seat, and finally upon a single roundel of well-designed ornament carved on its splat to give it its marked individuality. For balance, and to pull down the back, the stretcher binding the two rear legs has been placed below the level of the side ones, not above them. If there were no superstructure, the splayed lower portion of this piece would be much like a strongly made, solid stool. The line of the head rail, with its double break, crowns the whole; without this the chair would lose much of its character. The general effect is one of almost botanical freedom of upward curvature, yet with a strong, capping termination.

Wood: *Nan-mu*

Full height	3 feet, 7 inches
Breadth	1 foot, 6¾ inches
Depth	1 foot, 3¼ inches
Height to seat	1 foot, 7 inches

In the possession of Miss Mildred Walker.

88 ## SQUARE STOOL

This is a stool with a top made of a single solid piece of wood, the edges of which have been well rounded. Bracketed aprons between the simple dowel legs and plain dowel stretchers are the only other elements of the design. Given its small size, and general effect of portability, it may serve as a convenient point of departure for a consideration of the range in general. Even in an unpretentious stool like this the splay of the legs gives a sense of great functional stability. One feels, also, that the piece will withstand hard wear and give long service.

Wood: *Huang hua-li*

Height	1 foot, 7½ inches
Width	1 foot, 4 inches
Depth	1 foot, 4 inches

In the possession of Dr. Gustav Ecke.

89   SQUARE STOOL

Here the profiling of the framework, encasing a slightly sunken square of finely woven matting, increases the refinement of the type; and the horse-hoof legs, with a slight bead, merge at the top in the usual single surface with the apron. The stretchers are also of a familiar type which invariably gives a lightening effect to the lines of the construction. This is a useful piece of furniture, taking its place admirably in the traditional setting. It is classic in type and arrangement, and in its perfect proportioning.

Wood: *Huang hua-li*

Height	1 foot, 7 inches
Width	1 foot, 5 inches
Depth	1 foot, 5 inches

In the possession of Dr. Gustav Ecke.

90   SQUARE STOOL

Here tne stool is seen taking on scale and solidity, and moldings are multiplied in number. Notice the design of the legs: quarter round, in section, for the outside quadrant, changing to a right angle, with two flat surfaces, within. This, with variants, is a not uncommon arrangement. It should also be observed that each member of the openwork framing, three rectangles to each side, is doubled, although through good use of scale, there is no overemphasis on detail. As in the preceding example, and as is frequently to be seen in table construction, the legs and one horizontal surface under the top are run together. A collar is then placed above; giving to the acutal top an effect not unlike the tripartite arrangement of the moldings of a classical cornice.

Wood: *Huang hua-li*

Height	1 foot, $7\frac{3}{4}$ inches
Width	1 foot, 8 inches
Depth	1 foot, 8 inches

In the possession of Dr. Gustav Ecke.

91   SQUARE STOOL

Another example with a slightly sunken cane seat within a border
of hardwood. This piece was undoubtedly planned for a slightly
more ornate setting, so its beaded cloud heads here are doubled,
although their involuted ornament leaves the outline completely
uncluttered. In contrast with the plain rounded legs—squared on
the inner surfaces—the struts are beveled, and have been delicately
hollowed, catching the light and taking on living flexibility. The
usual slight splay perfects the balance; in these stools its effectiveness
can be apprehended at its simplest and best.

Wood: *Huang hua-li*

Height	1 foot, $7\frac{1}{2}$ inches
Width	1 foot, $10\frac{1}{4}$ inches
Depth	1 foot, $10\frac{1}{4}$ inches

In the possession of Miss C. F. Bieber.

92   OBLONG STOOL

A low stool, also with a cane seat, which shows how such a variant
could be planned wholly without moldings except for a very delicate
bead, using only such elements as those with which we are now
completely familiar. A set of oblong stools could be used as a change
from square ones where an effect of slightly individual elegance
was desired. The design relies for its effectiveness wholly upon good
proportioning; it would be difficult to make it in any way simpler
than it is.

Wood: *Huang hua-li*

Height	1 foot, $5\frac{1}{4}$ inches
Length	2 feet, $1\frac{3}{4}$ inches
Width	1 foot, $1\frac{1}{4}$ inches

In the possession of Messrs. Robert and William Drummond.

93 SMALL STAND

This elegant little example may possibly have served as a square, very low, *k'ang* table; yet it was more probably a stand designed for some precious object. The top, which is of a single thickness, the legs, and the low stretchers are all in one continuous plane. The feet have been reduced to unobstrusive hoofs, merely to keep the piece slightly raised from the floor or perhaps from the pile of a thick carpet.

If this were a stand—and they come in every possible size—to heighten Chinese pleasure in some object especially prized, it is quite possible that it was placed upon another surface such as a larger table top. From the heaviest bronze to the smallest vase, it was considered proper, in the old tradition, to give any object of quality this respectful elevation. The best examples, of the finest wood obtainable and made brilliant by much waxing and rubbing, in their refinement of design form almost a category of their own; although the most esteemed materials are still the blackwood and rosewood used for the best furniture making.

The soft rounding of corners, called *mo chiao,* or "rubbed corner" —or when large in scale, as we have seen, eel corner—often make it possible, as in this example, to dispense with moldings. Chinese taste is acutely conscious of the many ways in which transitions from one surface to another can be smoothly effected; and one seldom sees a hard angle.

Wood: *Hung-mu*

Height	11¼ inches
Width	1 foot, 5¼ inches
Depth	1 foot, 5¼ inches

In the possession of Miss C. F. Bieber.

NOTE:

We have now examined traditional examples of a variety of pieces, with legs and a top surface, whether to accommodate objects to be set upon them or to be used by people. These are all part of the very human business of obtaining release from uncivilized crawling and sprawling, to move about in more space and with more order and freedom. We continue and conclude the general types of table design by giving a number of variants of different heights and for different purposes, some more ornamental than the foregoing, yet all with legs and a flat top.

94   TABLE

A stand, or table, which shows the possibilities of design with simple traditional elements, such as the oblique strut and horse-hoof feet, already often seen. The extra base, a flat frame to which the legs themselves were made fast, is often of less precious wood than the piece it supported, and is not at all an unfamiliar feature. One of its uses was to prevent damage from dampness. For another example of this additional flat frame, see that placed below the Chinese ice chest in Plate 105. Pieces such as this might be used for porcelain jars filled with blooming plants or, in very elegant interiors, for vases filled with precious ornaments, such as branches of coral, lacquered *ju-i* scepters, etc.

Wood: *Huang hua-li*

Height	2 feet, 9½ inches
Length	1 foot, 9½ inches
Width	1 foot, 7 inches

Formerly in the possession of the late Mr. Pollard d'Urquhart.

95   SMALL TABLE

In China miscellaneous tables of all sizes, shapes, and heights are legion. This is an example of a small decorated one with rounded corners on both framework and fretwork, yet with the basic design wholly rectilinear. Such frets with rubbed corners are a device that in China must go back to great antiquity, and yet the motifs of this repertory, through the centuries, never seem to have lost their effectiveness. Lines of light are secured by making members slightly concave, and the breaks in the low stretchers are very effective. This small table is a variety often used in a group of three, set between two chairs. Guests rested their cups of tea on it, sitting in what is to Westerners a rather stiff position, at right angles beside it. To make symmetry perfect, each of such groups was, whenever possible, further balanced, across a room, by one identical with it.

Wood: *Huang hua-li*

Height	2 feet, 5¾ inches
Length	1 foot, 6 inches
Width	11 inches

In the possession of Dr. Gustav Ecke.

96   OCTAGONAL TABLE

The Chinese are adept in the use of the octagon, a geometric figure of which they are exceedingly fond. All the uprights of this example are framed, top and bottom, so as to make virtually open panels, resting on a base that goes around all eight sides. There are, thus, practically no proper legs; for although slight horse hoofs are used, all is held in place by the strong lower frame. At the very bottom, pieces of unobstrusive blocking, extending a little beyond the oblique sides, keep this frame from the floor. The whole design seems to be derived from an early type of structure. The moldings of the table top proper diminish as they go upward to form a collar, above which they project again to terminate in a solid, strong top. As so often, there is just enough surrender to fantasy in the ornamenting of the aprons to avoid dullness.

Wood: *Hung-mu*

Height	2 feet, 10½ inches
Diameter	1 foot, 6¾ inches

In the possession of M. Jean-Pierre Dubosc.

97   SMALL TABLE

A very solid model, in unusually lustrous wood, which is enriched with the full effect of many moldings, duplicating most of its lines and emphasizing them with repeated concave surfaces. This may possibly have been an incense table, to be furnished with a set of the usual implements, seen in so many formal ancestor portraits where one is usually placed near the sitter's chair or throne; its formality would be in perfect harmony with such a use. Yet it is not so high as these often were, and perhaps was designed merely for a setting in which great elegance of this type was desired.

Wood: *Hua-li*

Height	2 feet, 9¼ inches
Length	1 foot, 5¼ inches
Width	1 foot, 5¼ inches

In the possession of Miss C. F. Bieber.

98   SMALL CABINET

This is a piece of furniture of the people, more elaborate than
much we have hitherto seen, as if cheerfully to call attention to
itself. Many similar pieces were a part of the equipment of the itinerant barber, the riveter, or the tinker, or they were used for any one
of the many small trades that were carried on in the streets and
lanes, or under "mat sheds" at fairs. This cabinet was probably not
for ambulatory use, however, since such pieces were usually arranged
for suspension and ease of carriage from a shoulder pole. A similar
type also exists for the counters of small shops or for apothecaries'
wares, and its many small drawers would also fit it for certain uses
in a domestic setting.

Wood: *Yü-mu*

Height	1 foot, 6¾ inches
Width	2 feet, 8¼ inches
Depth	1 foot, ½ inch

In the possession of Miss C. F. Bieber.

99   LOW CHEST

Here is another piece in much the same style, included lest by
omission of this type the erroneous impression might be given that
all Chinese furniture was plain. A traditional design, it is executed
with great freedom, and each of its three drawers, it should be noticed,
is carved with a different floral motif. The notched and scalloped
ornament at the base is typical, as are also the spreading flanges at
the sides. This is a piece conceived in a tradition still deep in the
hearts of Chinese country people.

Wood: *Yü-mu*

Height	1 foot, 4½ inches
Breadth	3 feet, 9¾ inches
Depth	1 foot, 3 inches

In the possession of M. Jean-Pierre Dubosc.

100   SMALL K'ANG TABLE

A piece to show how well unpretentious small furniture for miscellaneous uses was worked out in the common idiom. This is
probably a child's desk, durable rather than elegant, its single drawer
to be used for books and writing materials. School children learned
their first lessons by heart, often together on a large k'ang, especially
among the humbler classes in the North. The piece is low, strong,
and obviously made to withstand hard usage. Like many tables
destined for popular use, it also has a certain amount of ornament
in a deeply traditional style, all of it simple and sturdy. Chicken-
wing wood is an excellent material for a piece of this kind.

Wood: *Chi-ch'ih-mu*

Height	1 foot, 1½ inches
Length	2 feet, 2 inches
Width	1 foot, 7¼ inches
In the possession of Miss C. F. Bieber.	

101   MIRROR STAND

This frame, now used for a small mirror, may originally have
been for an ornamental table screen; modern glass with mercury
backing, a Western invention, came to China only late in her history.
The arrangement, however, is the traditional one for screens which,
in the largest sizes, were practically big enough to form partitions
between rooms. This piece is included because it suggests how the
problem of the mirror, indispensable for us in so many surroundings, can successfully be handled within the repertory of native
Chinese design.

Wood: *Hua-li*

Height	2 feet, 5¼ inches
Width	2 feet, 10 inches
Depth at base	1 foot, ½ inch
In the possession of Dr. Gustav Ecke.	

102   SMALL CHEST

Smaller containers of every possible size and shape, and ingenious
combinations of cupboards and drawers, also exist. There are end-

less combinations. Many of the examples found today were originally ordered for some now-forgotten purpose, to satisfy personal wishes.

Here is one example in the form of a miniature chest of drawers, unpretentious and useful. It may have been used for a variety of minor objects—materials for fine embroidery, beads, seed pearls, tiny pieces of jade, etc., or brushes, ink-sticks, seals, and other small appurtenances for the writing or painting table. It has no locks, but seems reinforced with metal strips. These with its small, pendant, fish-tailed drawer pulls now give it part of its character.

Wood: *Huang hua-li*

Height	$8\frac{1}{4}$ inches
Width	1 foot, $3\frac{3}{4}$ inches
Depth	$9\frac{1}{2}$ inches

In the possession of Miss C. F. Bieber.

103 DRESSING CASE

A classic example of a hardwood dressing case, to be studied for its perfect handling of geometric problems. The unadorned solid block of the whole is relieved only by the cutout member finishing the supporting base, its small, well-swung ogee curves sensitively outlined with a strong bead. This base is attached, not separate, and its corners are reinforced with metal. Adding a single note of elaboration to the plain squares and single large round of the hardware above are the openwork drops that serve as door pulls. In spite of their small size, these give accents of distinction to the whole piece.

Wood: *Huang hua-li*

Height	1 foot, $3\frac{3}{4}$ inches
Width	1 foot, $5\frac{1}{4}$ inches
Depth	1 foot, $2\frac{3}{4}$ inches

In the possession of Miss Mildred Walker.

104 DRESSING CASE

This, like the foregoing, is probably a variety of dressing case which was used under the old regime by officials to store court beads or buttons of rank, belt buckles, and other objects for ceremonial use. It would thus be the male counterpart of the similar, though usually smaller and narrower, "missy box," so often sold to tourists, which is usually equipped with a modern mirror folded easel-like under the lid. The top is hinged at the back and lifts up, thus allowing the two small doors to open. Within there is a traylike compartment, placed under the cover, and usually several varieties of small drawers below. The shape and the placing of the hardware in this example, as usual, give richness to the design.

Wood: *Huang hua-li*

Height	1 foot, 4½ inches
Width	1 foot, 3 inches
Depth	11¾ inches

In the possession of Messrs. Robert and William Drummond.

105   ICE CHEST

This is a Chinese icebox, used to contain a block of ice in its pewter-lined chest, which served to cool refreshments, or to store fruit and flowers, in warm weather. Very large, almost giant, models of this same type were also placed in the apartments of the Summer Palace, as late as the time of the last Empress Dowager, merely to freshen the air when she was in residence. As can be seen in the plate, the cover is simply made of a pair of openwork boards which were removable. The interior is also pierced so that a pottery vessel could be placed below for drainage. There is great strength in the outline of the separate horsehoof legged stand, with its own additional frame making a further base to keep off damp. Besides the use of several varieties of wood, a rich polychromatic effect is obtained by the juxtaposition of no less than three metals: pewter in the stripping at the top under the cover, and a combination of brass with copper for the reinforcing bands and the handles.

Woods: *Pai-mu* sides; *hsiang sha-mu* cover; *li-mu* stand

Height	2 feet, 1 inch
Width	1 foot, 6 inches
Depth	1 foot, 6 inches

In the possession of Mr. George N. Kates.

106   FUR CHEST

As a result of the China trade, chests of every size and shape early made their way to Europe and America; indeed many of them seem to have been fabricated *ad hoc,* with much extraneous and inferior decoration. In the West this typical, absolutely plain, variety is comparatively rare. It is known as a *t'ang hsiang,* or "lying chest," for putting away heavy garments of fur, or with fur linings, in which transverse folds were to be avoided. Camphorwood was preferred for the best examples, yet other plain woods were also used, usually in an attempt to imitate the former. The hollow base, which forms a separate piece, kept the chest proper away from the damp of the floor. It should be noted that in the present example this base alone is ornamented; the chest itself, except for padlock shield and handles, relies for its effect solely upon good proportioning and the grain of excellent wood.

Wood: *Chang-mu*

Height	2 feet, ¾ inch
Width	4 feet, 1¼ inches
Depth	2 feet, ¾ inch

In the possession of Miss C. F. Bieber.

107   CLOTHES RACK

This is a Chinese clothes rack, elaborate in carving yet fundamentally a simple piece. Representations are often seen in genre painting. They were used to lay out and keep conveniently in order layers of clothing discarded or prepared for later wearing, and the use of them seems to have been evidence that an installation was considered luxurious. The Chinese are fastidious about changing the weight of their clothing with changing temperature, and since all their clothes are easily folded, this was also a practical piece. The lowest level was for footwear; smaller articles could be placed on the two rails above; and heavier, full-length garments were thrown over the top, where they were held in place by the projecting endpieces.

Wood: *Huang hua-li*

Height	5 feet, 6½ inches
Width	4 feet, 6 inches
Depth at Base	1 foot, 6½ inches

In the possession of Dr. Gustav Ecke.

108   WASH STAND

This stand for a washbasin has been somewhat altered for later adaptation to Western use; a mirror was added under the carving in the upper rectangle and one inset panel just below this was removed. It has apparently lost two external brackets, probably with flangelike profiling, supporting the top bar terminated with the dragons' heads. The framework, however, is unchanged. Quite remarkable is the considerable height of this piece and the pronounced entasis of the two uprights at the back. The support for the basin is of strong, yet light, geometric construction, and the hexagon makes an ideal figure for this purpose. Towels could also conveniently be flung over the top rail so that this is a useful as well as a decorative piece.

Wood: *Huang hua-li*

Full height	5 feet, 9¾ inches
Height to top of wash basin	2 feet, 3½ inches
Diameter	2 feet, ¾ inches

In the possession of Mr. George N. Kates.

109   LAMP STAND

Although the Chinese never developed their arrangements for lighting beyond candles or fairly primitive lamps, they did devise quite elaborate means for having the flame, in an elegant interior, at a convenient height. The upright rod that supports the movable lantern base is fixed to a crosspiece that can be raised or lowered in its grooved stand at will; it is kept in place by a simple wedge as seen in the plate. Although fairly elaborate, as was considered fitting for a piece of this kind, the design is functionally practical.

Wood: *Huang hua-li*

Height to lantern	4 feet, 1½ inches
Width at base	11¾ inches
Depth at base	1 foot, 1¾ inches
In the possession of Dr. Gustav Ecke.	

110   LAMP STAND

Here is another type of lamp stand which makes use of the same principle. It is not likely that the horn lanterns used on both of these examples were the original installation; this was more probably a metal sesame oil lamp or a pewter pricket candlestick. As in the preceding example, a small wedge-shaped piece of wood keeps the upright at whatever height it is set. These adjustable stands, it should be remarked, like most Chinese objects were usually made in pairs. They were decorative adjuncts to add a note of finish to their setting.

Wood: *Huang hua-li*

Height to lantern	3 feet, 11 inches
Width at base	10½ inches
Depth at base	11½ inches
In the possession of Messrs. Robert and William Drummond.	

111   LANTERN

Hanging lanterns gave the Chinese many opportunities to satisfy their fondness for decorative illumination, especially when porches or porticoes were adorned with large numbers of them for such prolonged festivities as those of the New Year. Although many were of gaudy or rather impermanent materials, as can so often be seen in representations in painting, good hardwood was also occasionally used; then, as in the accompanying plate, details were directly related to furniture design.

Wood: *Huang hua-li*

Full height	1 foot, 11 inches
Height of panels	1 foot, 3½ inches
Width of panels	6¾ inches
In the possession of Messrs. Robert and William Drummond.	

112 LANTERN

Here is a sensitively conceived, sober design of hardwood for another lantern. Its various members have close similarities to details in pieces of furniture already illustrated, and there is the same instinctive sense of what is required for proper handling of problems of volume. In this example all is intentionally further refined to extreme lightness. The result is an object distinctively Chinese, admirably adapted to its use.

Wood: *Huang hua-li*

Full height	2 feet, 3 inches
Height of panels	1 foot, 7½ inches
Width of panels	1 foot, 2½ inches
In the possession of Dr. Gustav Ecke.	

NOTES TO THE WOODCUTS
IN THE TEXT

SUMMARY WORKING BIBLIOGRAPHY

Apart from the eighteenth-century works mentioned in Notes to the Text, inaccurate but early, the following may prove of use. They represent, in chronological order, practically all the books and chief articles of real value that have appeared on Chinese furniture in Western languages. As may be seen, the list is not very extensive.

ROCHE, ODILON, *Les Meubles de la Chine.*
    Paris: A. Calavas, N. D. (*cir.* 1921).
    (A German edition titled, *Chinesische Möbel.* Stuttgart: Julius Hoffman, 1924.)

CESCINSKY, HERBERT. *Chinese Furniture.* London: Benn Bros., 1922.

DUPONT, MAURICE. *Les Meubles de la Chine.* (*Deuxième Série*). Paris: A. Calavas, N. D. (1926).

SLOMANN, WILHELM. "*Chinesische Möbel des 18. Jahrhunderts,*" *Pantheon,* March, 1929, pp. 142–148.

ECKE, GUSTAV, "*Sechs Schaubilder Pekinger Innenraeume des Achtzehnten Jahrhunderts,*" *Bulletin* No. 9, Catholic University of Peking, November, 1934, pp. 155–169.

FERGUSON, JOHN C., "*Chinese Furniture,*" *T'ien Hsia Monthly,* March, 1937, pp. 246–253. Also as Chap. VIII, pp. 109–115, with plates, in his *Survey of Chinese Art.* Shanghai: The Commercial Press, 1940.

ECKE, GUSTAV. "*Wandlungen des Faltstuhls, Bemerkungen zur Geschichte der Eurasischen Stuhlform,*" *Monumenta Serica,* IX (1944), pp. 34–52.

ECKE, GUSTAV. *Chinese Domestic Furniture.* Peking: Editions Henri Vetch, 1944.

A CATALOGUE OF
SELECTED DOVER BOOKS
IN ALL FIELDS OF INTEREST

A CATALOGUE OF SELECTED DOVER
BOOKS IN ALL FIELDS OF INTEREST

CELESTIAL OBJECTS FOR COMMON TELESCOPES, T. W. Webb. The most used book in amateur astronomy: inestimable aid for locating and identifying nearly 4,000 celestial objects. Edited, updated by Margaret W. Mayall. 77 illustrations. Total of 645pp. 5⅜ x 8½.
20917-2, 20918-0 Pa., Two-vol. set $9.00

HISTORICAL STUDIES IN THE LANGUAGE OF CHEMISTRY, M. P. Crosland. The important part language has played in the development of chemistry from the symbolism of alchemy to the adoption of systematic nomenclature in 1892. ". . . wholeheartedly recommended,"—Science. 15 illustrations. 416pp. of text. 5⅝ x 8¼.   63702-6 Pa. $6.00

BURNHAM'S CELESTIAL HANDBOOK, Robert Burnham, Jr. Thorough, readable guide to the stars beyond our solar system. Exhaustive treatment, fully illustrated. Breakdown is alphabetical by constellation: Andromeda to Cetus in Vol. 1; Chamaeleon to Orion in Vol. 2; and Pavo to Vulpecula in Vol. 3. Hundreds of illustrations. Total of about 2000pp. 6⅛ x 9¼.
23567-X, 23568-8, 23673-0 Pa., Three-vol. set $26.85

THEORY OF WING SECTIONS: INCLUDING A SUMMARY OF AIR-FOIL DATA, Ira H. Abbott and A. E. von Doenhoff. Concise compilation of subatomic aerodynamic characteristics of modern NASA wing sections, plus description of theory. 350pp. of tables. 693pp. 5⅜ x 8½.
60586-8 Pa. $7.00

DE RE METALLICA, Georgius Agricola. Translated by Herbert C. Hoover and Lou H. Hoover. The famous Hoover translation of greatest treatise on technological chemistry, engineering, geology, mining of early modern times (1556). All 289 original woodcuts. 638pp. 6¾ x 11.
60006-8 Clothbd. $17.95

THE ORIGIN OF CONTINENTS AND OCEANS, Alfred Wegener. One of the most influential, most controversial books in science, the classic statement for continental drift. Full 1966 translation of Wegener's final (1929) version. 64 illustrations. 246pp. 5⅜ x 8½.   61708-4 Pa. $4.50

THE PRINCIPLES OF PSYCHOLOGY, William James. Famous long course complete, unabridged. Stream of thought, time perception, memory, experimental methods; great work decades ahead of its time. Still valid, useful; read in many classes. 94 figures. Total of 1391pp. 5⅜ x 8½.
20381-6, 20382-4 Pa., Two-vol. set $13.00

AMERICAN ANTIQUE FURNITURE, Edgar G. Miller, Jr. The basic coverage of all American furniture before 1840: chapters per item chronologically cover all types of furniture, with more than 2100 photos. Total of 1106pp. 7⅞ x 10¾.   21599-7, 21600-4 Pa., Two-vol. set $17.90

ILLUSTRATED GUIDE TO SHAKER FURNITURE, Robert Meader. Director, Shaker Museum, Old Chatham, presents up-to-date coverage of all furniture and appurtenances, with much on local styles not available elsewhere. 235 photos. 146pp. 9 x 12.   22819-3 Pa. $5.00

ORIENTAL RUGS, ANTIQUE AND MODERN, Walter A. Hawley. Persia, Turkey, Caucasus, Central Asia, China, other traditions. Best general survey of all aspects: styles and periods, manufacture, uses, symbols and their interpretation, and identification. 96 illustrations, 11 in color. 320pp. 6⅛ x 9¼.   22366-3 Pa. $6.95

CHINESE POTTERY AND PORCELAIN, R. L. Hobson. Detailed descriptions and analyses by former Keeper of the Department of Oriental Antiquities and Ethnography at the British Museum. Covers hundreds of pieces from primitive times to 1915. Still the standard text for most periods. 136 plates, 40 in full color. Total of 750pp. 5⅝ x 8½.
23253-0 Pa. $10.00

THE WARES OF THE MING DYNASTY, R. L. Hobson. Foremost scholar examines and illustrates many varieties of Ming (1368-1644). Famous blue and white, polychrome, lesser-known styles and shapes. 117 illustrations, 9 full color, of outstanding pieces. Total of 263pp. 6⅛ x 9¼. (Available in U.S. only)   23652-8 Pa. $6.00

Prices subject to change without notice.

Available at your book dealer or write for free catalogue to Dept. GI, Dover Publications, Inc., 180 Varick St., N.Y., N.Y. 10014. Dover publishes more than 175 books each year on science, elementary and advanced mathematics, biology, music, art, literary history, social sciences and other areas.